Australian Sugar Artistry

Australian Sugar Artistry

Marian Jones

JBFP

A J.B. Fairfax Publication

DEDICATION

To my ever patient husband Neville who made numerous trips to and from the airport to pick up the marvellous creations of sugar art that invariably arrived in Sydney at some ungodly hour and then chauffeured me and them to the photographer without further mishap.

To my late mother and father who both encouraged me long ago to return to my cake decorating and to Carol Jacobson my long-suffering editor who pulled my vision into a wonderful production. Thank you.

Marian Jones

Published by J.B. Fairfax Press Pty Limited
80-82 McLachlan Avenue
Rushcutters Bay
Sydney, NSW 2011 Australia
A.C.N. 003 738 430

Editorial and Production
Managing Editor: Rachel Blackmore
Production Manager: Anna Maguire

This book was designed and produced by
Electronic Publishing Solutions
44 Stone Parade
Davidson, NSW 2085 Australia
A.C.N. 053 996 526

Editor
Carol Jacobson

Design
Electronic Publishing Solutions

Photography
Fretwell Photography Pty Limited

Illustrations
Wild Red Frog Design

Printed by Toppan Printing Co, Singapore
Printed in Singapore

JBFP 362
AUSTRALIAN SUGAR ARTISTRY
Includes Index
ISBN 1 86343 199 3

Half title: This elegant swan is made using the sugar blowing method. The ribbon is made from pulled sugar. (See page 65.)
Title page: This exquisite wedding cake was the gold medal winner at the 9th FHA Salon Culinaire. (See page 168.)

Contents

These superb flamingoes are formed from stiffened tulle which is piped all over in cornelli work. *(See page 118.)*
Opposite: The three tiers of this unusual wedding cake are made inside croquembouche tins. *(See page 182.)*

CONTRIBUTORS

Dorothy Allison
Donna Baldock
Barbara Batterham
Hervé Boutin
Rosemary Bruce-Mullins
Wilma Bursac
Jean Cole-Clark
Gail Gambrell
Adèle Humphrys
Marian Jones
Julia Kook
Linda McGlinn
Mavis Mepham
Jean Palmer
Eileen Scriven
Lynette Speer
Kath Swansbra
Lorraine Wells
Carol Wright

INTRODUCTION

ith great pleasure I present this book to you. It has long been a dream of mine to show the world the talent that abounds among our cake decorators here in Australia. We have many sugar artists that are already well known and need no introduction, but a lot of our very talented people remain unseen. They enter shows and competitions; sometimes their magnificent creations appear in publications but most often they do not and I have always thought they deserve to be on show.

The list of contributors is by no means definitive but is representative of the tremendous talent in Australia. The cooperation of these people in making each piece and preparing it for shipping is greatly appreciated. I would especially like to thank those who had to remake or repair items that were damaged in transit.

The logistics involved in getting the displays to our very professional photographers Robert and Anthony Fretwell were horrendous. Australia is so huge and air transport is unreliable for safe delivery of such delicate and intricate displays. But many patient hours later we achieved what I consider to be a truly great display of our Australian artists and I hope their skills will become part of our heritage.

Marian Jones

SECTION ONE

FLOODWORK

BRUSH FLOOD

RUN-IN FLOOD

BACK-TO-BACK FLOOD

Fairies • Lace • Embroidery

FAIRIES FLOODWORK

Carol Wright

he fairies are made using floodwork in back-to-back technique combined with some piping and moulding. They are then positioned carefully amongst the spray of sweet pea flowers.

First prepare the design for the fairies. Each section of every major piece should be made separately and joined later. It is best to draw or trace the complete picture and then divide it into logical sections. For the fairies I made the torso first. I then made the legs and arms followed by the skirt, wings and finally the face.

After you have chosen the design, trace out the different sections. Secure the pattern on a flat surface and cover with non-stick transparent paper or baking paper making sure that there are no creases.

Use a no. 1 or 0 piping tube and pipe the outline of the torso. Flood and fill the torso with fresh royal icing. Use a moist brush to achieve the desired shaping. Pipe separately all the sections of the figure that will add an extra dimension to the piece.

Make the legs separately and when dry attach to the torso. Make the arms next with the sleeves attached. When dry attach them to the torso with royal icing.

Make the skirt in four pieces. The front, side and back pieces are flooded separately and attached to the torso when dry. The top piece is piped on last of all.

Make the face, hat and the wings from moulding paste. Allow to dry and then paint. Attach the face, hat and one wing to the body with royal icing. Allow to dry.

When the fairy is dry carefully remove from the paper and turn over and complete the back of the fairy as for the front. After the back is dry, add the second wing and pipe on the fourth section of the skirt. Allow to dry thoroughly.

Paint the features, shading and other details with a fine paint brush and food colour.

Combine the fairies with the sweet peas, leaves and the tendrils, keeping the whole arrangement soft and light. Carefully attach the spray to the covered cake using a little royal icing.

The tiny fairies have sweet pea skirts and hats. Their faces are moulded and then combined with the flowers. *(See page 171.)*

SWEET PEA BRUSH FLOODWORK

Carol Wright

he brush floodwork used here gives a delicate raised look to the simple side design. The result is exquisite.

For this type of brush floodwork the outline of the design is piped and then each section is filled with soft peak royal icing to which a small amount of piping gel is added. This will delay the drying process allowing more time for the icing to be brushed into place using a damp brush dipped in the same mixture. It is important that the brush is only slightly damp and it is usually necessary to squeeze the brush a little to remove any excess moisture.

Usually brush floodwork is done with white icing with the colour painted on later. Using colour in royal icing mix can create an uneven finish when using a damp brush. The cake is covered and later placed on a covered board. Any finishing border for the base of the cake must be piped on before any additional floodwork, lace or extension work is added.

Make a paper pattern for the side design. Secure the pattern to a flat surface and cover with non-stick transparent paper or baking paper. Tape down firmly. Always work from the background to the foreground. Use a no. 1 or 0 piping tube to pipe the outline of the background petal.

Choose a good quality sable brush for your brush floodwork. Prepare the royal icing to a soft peak consistency and dip the brush in water. Squeeze out the excess moisture and dip lightly into the icing.

Use the damp brush to brush the icing towards the centre of the petal. Leave the icing thicker where the petals overlap or the edges are furled. Continue in this way until you have reached the front of the design, piping and brushing each petal in turn.

Allow each section to dry before continuing. The final effect can be smooth or rough depending on the way you use the brush. When the pattern is dry carefully remove from the non-stick paper. If the design is fragile or too large it can be removed in sections and joined carefully when attaching to the cake. Pipe a series of dots on the back of the floodwork to suspend and secure it from the side of the cake. Put in position and allow to dry. Any extra extension work or lace can then be added to complete the cake border.

The sweet pea design is made separately and attached to the cake with royal icing. The finished effect lifts off the surface and gives lightness to the design. *(See page 171.)*

MAGNOLIA BRUSH FLOODWORK

Carol Wright

magnolia pattern in brush floodwork is combined here with delicate extension work to give continuity to this wedding cake. A brush is used to push the icing into the outline giving a more raised result than traditional flat flooding with a piping tube.

Prepare the cake, cover and place on a covered board. Choose the floodwork design, ensuring that it complements any flowers or other decoration you are putting on the cake. Draw the pattern and lay it against the cake to make sure it is the right size. Secure the pattern to the side of the tin in which the cake was cooked. This will ensure that the curve of the floodwork matches exactly the curve of the cake. Cover with non-stick transparent paper or baking paper.

Prepare royal icing to a soft peak and do not precolour because the use of a damp brush to move the icing will cause an uneven flow of colour. Brush floodwork must be painted when dry.

Beginning with the background, pipe the outline of the design using a no. 1 or 0 piping tube. Do one section at a time.

Take a good quality sable brush, dip in water and squeeze out any excess moisture. Dip very lightly in royal icing and gently brush the icing from edges to the centre. Continue in this way working from the back of the design to the foreground. Allow the whole piece to dry thoroughly.

Any finishing border for the base of the cake must be piped on before applying additional floodwork, lace or extension work to the sides.

Carefully remove the piece from the paper. If the design is large it can be carefully divided into two or more pieces which are later joined on the cake. Extra pieces can be flooded and added to the design so that they flow over onto the board. It is these touches that give a design that something extra.

Pipe a series of tiny dots of royal icing on the back. These will hold it in position on the cake and also keep it off the surface just a little and bring the whole design to life.

Place in position on the cake and allow to dry. When thoroughly dry it's time to add any extension work, lace or flowers that you wish.

The curve of the floodwork is obtained by making the pieces on the outside of the tin in which the cake was cooked.
(See page 187.)

MOUSE AND CHEESE

Carol Wright

his novelty piece is constructed using a number of cake decorating techniques. The mouse is made using back-to-back floodwork, the crackers and cheese were cut from moulding paste and the cheese board dome was made from gelatine.

The first step is to make the cheese board dome. Choose a good smooth mould. Gelatine mixture is fussy stuff and is quite selective about what it will stick to. Perspex or plastic is usually the best. The mixture tends to come loose from glass before setting and can often turn cloudy when moulded on a balloon.

Prepare a warm gelatine mixture and pour into the mould. Temperature is fairly important—if it is too hot or too cold the mixture will not stick to the mould. The handle of the dome was formed over a small balloon dipped in the gelatine mixture. Leave the dome and handle to dry for three to four days.

Pop the balloon inside the handle and remove carefully. Remove the dome from the mould and neaten the edge. Take extreme care at this stage because the gelatine is brittle and tends to split. Attach the handle to the dome with gum arabic glue.

Prepare the design for the mouse. Pipe the outline of the first section and then flood keeping the piping tube under the surface until the desired plumpness is achieved. Carefully remove the tube without leaving a tiny trail. Smooth out the icing with a slightly damp brush. Leave to dry. Repeat for all other sections.

Turn over all the mouse parts and repeat the outlining and flooding process on the back of each piece. Leave to completely dry and then colour using a good quality brush. Let each colour dry thoroughly before continuing.

Make a batch of moulding paste and cut out the crackers. Form a wedge of Cheddar from moulding paste. Leave to dry and then colour these pieces. Assemble the parts on a base to resemble a cheese board.

This piece won first prize in the Sugarcraft Section at the Queensland Agricultural Show.

Caught in the act, this tiny mouse is trapped under a gelatine dome. The cheese and crackers are made from moulding paste.

MINI CAKE PRESSURE FLOODING

Kath Swansbra

his mini cake—it only has a diameter of about 11 cm/4½ in—has an intricate continuous mural running around the sides and a romantic bouquet on top. The whole effect gives a 'Beatrix Potter' feel to the cake.

Prepare the cake, cover and place on a precovered board. Pipe a beading around the base to neaten the edge. Allow to dry.

To prepare a continuous design for a cake, first calculate the circumference of the cake. Measure this distance onto paper and then reduce or enlarge your design to fit the length. Transfer the pattern or mural to the cake.

Use soft to medium peak royal icing and a no. 0 piping tube. The exact texture of the icing depends on the size of the figure and the area you need to cover. Begin by piping the outline of the area that appears to be the background.

After outlining, use a circular motion to fill in the area. Do not remove the tube from the icing but leave the tip under the surface. Use extra pressure to build up the muscle or body and face shapes. Once the desired shape is achieved carefully remove the tube. Take care that there are no tails of icing when the tube is removed. Use a small brush to flatten them if they do occur.

This tiny cake is covered with flooded animals in a continuous mural. Each piece is hand painted in intricate detail.

Take your time and rotate the cake as you go. Complete all of the background pieces before beginning on the foreground. It is a good idea to complete similar sections of each piece and then go on to the next. For example, do all the bodies, then the legs, followed by the arms, etc. This will give a consistency to the design. Let some of the rocks and flowers flow onto the board to give a soft romantic look. The design should not be too rigid. Some of this effect will just happen as you go.

Continue in this manner all around the cake gradually building up the pattern.

Allow the mural to dry and then paint with food colour. Use a good quality brush and take your time. Paint all the sections of the one colour at the same time then change colour and work your way around the cake.

After completing all the pressure flooding and painting, it is time to adorn the design with elements that will add extra depth and interest. I have added flowers made from moulding paste as well as lace trims on the clothing. Tiny bows and fine ribbons are perfect to complete the design.

Finally it is time to make the top posy. The flowers are made from moulding paste. The choice of course is yours but I have used roses as the main flower. Tulle and ribbons are added to the sugar flowers to complete the bouquet.

Pipe a dainty lace trim around the top edge of the cake after placing the posy of tulle and flowers on top.

Opposite and this page: Each picture shows a different side panel on this tiny cake. The flooded pieces are finished with moulded flowers and buds.

GOLFER IN THE ROUGH

Wilma Bursac

his picture delighted me every time I looked at it and always beckoned me to get out the icing bag and make it. Eventually I did it and the result is a humorous cake that delights everyone.

Prepare the cake, cover it and place on a covered board. Draw or trace the design onto non-stick transparent paper. Place the paper on the cake and pin prick the design onto the cake. Next secure the pattern to a flat surface. This will be used to create the flooded pieces which will be added separately after all the background is completed.

Begin with the background and work towards the foreground. The background trees are painted on with liquid food colour. Allow to dry.

The main trees are flooded separately and then placed on the cake and any branches and leaves are added last. The squiggly branches, briar bushes in the front and the individual leaves and twigs are also piped or moulded then coloured before being attached to the cake with royal icing.

The live golfer is piped and flooded in royal icing, left to dry and then coloured. Paint the background colour on his jumper and pants and allow to dry completely before adding the ribbed and plaid pattern. Assemble the golfer with royal icing working from the torso then onto his legs, arms, head and hat.

This golfer is in for a shock when he goes looking for his lost ball. The design is a combination of flooded pieces with moulding, pipework and hand painting.

The circular weeds are fine stamens painted and bent in the middle. Tie a bunch with cotton then push open to get the circular effect required. Place the bunch onto the surface of the cake and hold in place with a little royal icing.

The dead golfer is piped separately in small bony lots, then piled together. Pipe the golf stick he is holding then add his fingers and hands. Allow to dry then fix the golf club to the tree trunk with royal icing. Hold at the right height until dry. Once it is dry add his forearms, from the wrist to the elbow, with a little royal icing.

The briars and brambles that the skeleton is sitting in are then assembled. This is quite a time consuming task as all the pieces are individually attached. When sufficient have been attached to achieve the bushy effect the skeleton's legs are put in place and then more bush is put around them. Place the lost golf ball in the tree above him.

Attach the ribbons around the sides with a little royal icing. Make a second skull using floodwork and paint on the bony pattern. Pipe the golf club and ball. Allow to dry and then attach these pieces to the side of the cake.

The golfer is assembled from flooded pieces, working from the torso, then legs, arms, head and hat.

A simple beaded edge and ribbon are all that are needed to finish this cake.

PLATYPUS AND CHRISTMAS WREATH CAKE

Wilma Bursac

s I am always on the lookout for an Australian Christmas theme I decided to create this design including a platypus combined with a traditional Christmas wreath and bow. Judging by the worried expression on his face he doesn't seem too happy about the idea but maybe it's just too much Christmas cheer.

I have kept the decorations on this cake simple and the colours very neutral but the whole appearance can be changed by colouring the wreath and using bright ribbons for the bow.

Prepare the cake, cover it with royal icing and place on a covered board. Draw or trace the pattern onto paper and cover with non-stick transparent paper or baking paper. Secure firmly to a flat surface. Draw or trace the paws and secure ready for flooding.

Use a no. 1 or 0 piping tube and royal icing to pipe the outline of the design. Flood the platypus from the centre gradually filling towards the edges. Smooth the edges with a fine brush and leave to dry for two days. Repeat this process for the paws.

When the platypus pieces are thoroughly dry paint them with liquid food colours. The painting takes considerable time but the effort is worth it. To give the coat its furry look, apply one colour at a time and allow it to dry thoroughly before beginning the next colour. The facial lines that give this little guy so much personality are applied after all the background colours are dry. Use a fine-tipped brush with a very steady hand. Paint the paws in the same way again allowing each colour to dry before proceeding.

The holly for the wreath is made with white moulding paste. Make the holly leaves in different sizes and leave to dry.

Place the platypus body in position on the cake using royal icing, then arrange the holly wreath around the platypus. Place the paws in position and arrange a few holly leaves on top of the paws. Pipe a few extra leaves and bits and pieces.

Keep the background plain to show off the platypus. Silver cachous are added to the centre of the holly arrangement.

Opposite: A very Australian Christmas is the theme here with a none-too-happy platypus hanging on a Christmas wreath.

ROOSTER AND FAMILY

Wilma Bursac

his picture came from a children's farm animals storybook. The design was made with relief floodwork. This method gives height and texture to the design.

For the rooster it is necessary to determine where the raised body sections, i.e. chest, wings, thighs, tail, cockscomb, and wattle—the floppy bit under its beak—are to go. These raised sections are all made separately before commencing to flood the picture.

The chest and wings are made from moulding paste shaped over the back of a teaspoon, and the thighs are constructed from moulding paste formed inside two measuring spoons. When making shapes to support a picture, try to use a mould that is the shape required for the raised area. The cockscomb and wattle are flooded separately. The comb has a small spike piped onto it when it is flooded so there is an anchor to set in the royal icing. The legs and each feather are also piped separately and attached later.

The legs and feathers are piped onto stamens to add strength. This prevents shattering if the pieces break and repairs are much easier. When dry, these sections are coloured ready for use. If any of the pieces are to be set at an angle make sure they are coloured on both sides.

The rooster is flooded with a soft peak royal icing over the moulding paste shapes made to heighten the wings, chest and legs. By achieving height this way there is less royal icing piped into the shape making the piece lighter and easier to handle with less drying time.

When all the pieces are ready to be assembled secure the pattern under non-stick transparent paper or baking paper on a firm surface.

The chest and wing pieces are assembled first. It may be necessary to break off a little bit to ensure they fit snugly together. To join, use a no. 2 piping tube with royal icing which is the consistency of honey. Next position the legs and the thighs in position. Flooding can also be applied around these sections to fill all the spaces.

Having positioned these raised sections, the rooster's head is flooded next, minus the comb. Smooth the icing with a damp brush then insert the cockscomb. Pipe a little royal icing over the join and smooth out. A tiny wedge of foam is then positioned under the comb to keep it at an angle. Remember, when positioning the pieces use the background picture to ensure the alignment is correct.

The remaining pieces of the rooster are then flooded from the head down, the wattle is attached under the beak, then

Relief floodwork is used to build up the individual parts of the rooster.

flooding is gradually applied up over the chest and wing and down over the thighs making sure that the proper proportion is maintained.

It is handy to have another copy of the design alongside the work so that comparisons can be made to keep height and position of the joins in true perspective.

The tail is piped next as a rounded area from which all the feathers seem to emerge, and then individual feathers are inserted into that area. The feathers at the back of the rooster are flat, but as the tail is built up the feathers can be set at angles by using other feathers or tiny foam wedges for support. There are about fifteen tail feathers per rooster.

Once all the feathers are positioned, ensure they are not pushed too far up the back. If necessary, pull them back a bit and use a damp brush to smooth the royal icing at the base of the tail.

Allow the rooster to dry. This should not take too long because the base of the design is dry before assembly. When the piece is completely dry it is ready to be coloured.

Colouring floodwork can either make or break the final result. Select three good brushes for painting—thick, medium and very fine. Always mix colours on a large white palette and try to complete the painting without washing the palette. Paint all the large areas first and allow each area to dry thoroughly. Use a fine brush to detail the picture.

Remember don't wash the palette until the floodwork is completed and assembled. If an accident occurs during the final stages patching is much simpler if you still have some of the original colour—it is almost impossible to mix and match another batch of colour.

SIDE DESIGN

The hen and chickens on the side were reduced to fit the side of the cake. The hen is flooded in one piece and tail feathers are inserted as the flooding reaches that end of the hen. Flood this piece on the side of the tin that the cake has been cooked in to ensure it exactly fits the curve of the cake.

BACKGROUND

The background shell grit and the decorating around the board is made from moulding paste in four different colours. Roll it out thinly and leave to dry in sheets. When dry roll again with a rolling pin to break up and mix the pieces together. Push through a large sieve to make sure that all pieces are about the same size.

Pattern for the rooster showing position of tail feathers.

A hen and chicks wander around the sides of this cake. The shell grit is made from moulding paste pushed through a sieve.

THREE HAPPY MICE

Carol Wright

he idea for this wisp of fantasy was adapted from a greeting card. I drew up each mouse, carefully considering how they would finally fit together and particularly where their feet and tails would have to be. I then reversed the drawings and drew the back so that I could achieve a realistic effect.

After preparing the design, secure on a flat surface and cover with non-stick transparent paper or baking paper.

Smooth out carefully and tape down ensuring that there are no creases.

To support and strengthen the tiny figures, lay a cocktail stick or wooden toothpick in the section and secure with royal icing. Using fresh royal icing, outline one section at a time with a no. 1 or 0 piping tube and then fill with icing. Use a moist paint brush to coax the icing into the shape.

Always pipe separately any sections of the design that will add extra dimensions, i.e. arms, legs, hands and feet. When dry, these are added to the design with royal icing.

Complete the front of each mouse and when dry, carefully turn over. Lay the mice in

A single piece of wire is threaded through the three mice to keep them secure.

position and place a length of very fine wire down the length of the three mice. The wire between mouse one and two is covered with moulding paste and becomes the tail. Pipe the reverse side the same way. When dry paint the features, shading and details with a fine brush and food colour.

Each mouse is completed before the piece is assembled. I added the finishing touches—the whiskers and noses, the teeth and tails and the hands and feet—last of all. Sweet peas are my favourite flowers so it was very easy to decide what to use to suspend the little fellows. The tendrils give the whimsical effect I was after. It was a fun piece to do.

It won first prize in the Sugarcraft Section of the Queensland Show.

The three tiny mice are made using the back-to-back floodwork technique.

GUIPURE LACE

Mavis Mepham

or centuries lace has been used as a finishing touch to fabric and is probably the most traditional decoration used in cake decorating. Most of the fine lace reproduced in cake decorating is fine and delicate and it is great to find a different technique that is more robust but still maintains the look of soft trimming. Guipure lace is a form of floodwork and can be achieved successfully even if you weren't born with 'surgeon's hands'.

To create guipure lace, draw or trace the pattern and secure onto a flat surface. Remember guipure lace is made up of thicker threads with no bridges joining the pieces. Rather each piece seems to rest against its neighbour. Cover the pattern with non-stick transparent paper or baking paper. Prepare a batch of soft royal icing—it should be somewhere near the consistency of honey because it is to be used for very fine floodwork.

Small panels of lace are topped by brush embroidery.

Using a no. 00 piping tube, pipe the outside line of one lace piece. Next pipe the inside line. Now pipe a line between these two. This line is usually a little thicker and therefore floods to the outside lines. Repeat this process with each lace piece and allow to dry.

Pipe dots on the outer edge to give the pieces a realistic look. Pipe the inside pattern of each piece. Allow to dry. Each piece is fixed to the cake using tiny dots of royal icing.

For a different result, half the pattern can be piped directly onto the cake then predried lace pieces added to give a very delicate effect.

FLOODED HEART LACE

Adèle Humphrys

he lace surrounds for this wedding cake have been made using a combination of traditional piped lace with a flooded centre. Each section of five pieces is slightly curved out from the cake giving a scalloped effect.

Draw or trace the design for the lace. Ensure that the design you choose has a section that can be flooded. To achieve the curved effect, choose a surface that has the desired curve for the lace. The side of a cake tin or large bottle is ideal. Cover with non-stick transparent paper and secure firmly.

Make a batch of royal icing to soft peak consistency. Using a no. 00 piping tube pipe along the lines of one section of lace. Now put the piping tube in the centre of the heart shape and fill with royal icing allowing it to flood to the edges. Keep the tube under the surface until the desired roundness is achieved. Withdraw the piping tube and try not to leave a trail of icing. Use a slightly damp brush to clean up any tails or untidy bits. Pipe a series of dots on the lower edge of each piece. Repeat this process on each lace piece and allow them to dry thoroughly.

Carefully remove each section of lace and turn over. Pipe a series of small dots on the end pieces and place on the cake. Each section will curve out from the surface.

Each five-part panel of lace is made separately over a curved surface and then positioned. *(See page 189.)*

FLANNEL FLOWER BRUSH EMBROIDERY

Eileen Scriven

Dainty brush embroidery has always been a favourite of mine because it is perfect for duplicating the lace on a wedding dress or similar. However, with this cake I was looking for a way to give the embroidery a realistic look. After much experimentation, I developed a method of combining brush embroidery with moulding paste shapes to give just the effect I was after. The combination gives a lightness to the design and lifts it off the surface of the cake.

Prepare the cake, cover it and place on a precovered board.

Choose the design and transfer it to the cake. This is best done by tracing the design on the back of the tracing paper, then placing it in position on the cake, right side up, and carefully retracing the design gently onto the cake.

Once the design is on the cake, prepare a batch of royal icing and add $^1/_2$ teaspoon piping gel. Using a no. 1 piping tube, pipe the outline of one background piece. Using a good quality tapered brush, gently stroke the icing from the edges towards the centre of the piece. The outer edge will remain thicker and the centre will fade out to a fine sugar coating. If you are doing leaves or flowers follow the veins and natural design of the leaf or flowers to give a realistic look. Sometimes a second piping line can be added before the brush work begins. This makes the piece stand out from the rest.

After completing the brush embroidery, use the pattern to cut out some flannel flowers and leaves from moulding paste. Gently roll these into place on the brushwork. Complete the design with the addition of piped flowers and stems. The whole design will appear to lift off the flat surface of the cake and come to life.

Patterns for gum blossoms, leaves and buds that are added to the flannel flower design.

Patterns for flannel flowers, leaves and buds.

The floodwork on this cake is a series of layers of flowers, buds and leaves built up all over the surface. *(See page 185.)*

BRUSH EMBROIDERY

Kath Swansbra

his cake has such an abundance of features that simple brush embroidery in a symmetrical pattern is used on the sides of each tier.

Draw up the pattern for the design and transfer it to the cake either by pin-pricks or careful use of charcoal. Use royal icing with a soft peak consistency and pipe the outline of the flower petals onto the cake one at a time always beginning with the background and working towards the front. Take a very fine good quality brush and dip in water. Squeeze as much water as you can from the brush and then draw the royal icing from the outline towards the centre of each petal. The outside edge will be thicker and it should be very sparse and barely fill the area. The idea is lightness not necessarily a heavy embossing. Continue in this way around each cake tier. Allow the whole design to dry thoroughly before colouring. If the royal icing is precoloured the damp brush usually streaks the icing and spoils the colour.

Floodwork is one of the first things done on the covered cake with all extension work and lace edges being applied after the flooding. Because the bottom tier of this cake is a lily pond it is necessary to pipe a lace edge around the pond after the flooding is completed. The remaining decorations can then be added.

Parts of the design can also be done off the cake, e.g. front petals and leaves. Use the same method as above but on non-stick paper. Allow to dry and then transfer the pieces into position on the cake. This method makes the flowers more delicate and adds lightness and proportion to the overall effect.

Opposite: The brush embroidery is very symmetrical on this cake in contrast to the wonderful waterlilies and rocks. *(See page 169.)*

SECTION TWO

EXTENSION WORK

BORDERS

LATTICE

RIBBON

Lace • Waterfalls • Scallops

DROP THREADWORK EXTENSION DETAIL

Barbara Batterham

ine extension work with a delicate lace edging and embroidery is the ultimate finish to a cake. It should be designed as part of the whole and not just added later to finish off the edge. The length and thickness of the threads must be decided with the other decoration in mind.

It takes a lot of practice to pipe the drop threads closely and evenly to complete the desired fine work. The secret is evenly spaced dead straight lines maintained in the chosen pattern around the whole cake. It is important that you are immediately in front of the area you are piping. Any angle will cause the drop threads to slant slightly which becomes very exaggerated as you work around the cake.

The consistency of the royal icing varies according to the type of drop threads you are piping. If the dropped threadwork is to be short the royal icing should be of soft peak consistency. Longer lines, which are more difficult, need to be done with a stiffer mixture of royal icing or they will

Both tiers have matching extension work with the floral decorations flowing down the cake. (See page 191.)

Fine drop threadwork panels are separated by dropped loops.

sag. To achieve the gossamer effect use a very fine piping tube such as a no. 000 or 00.

The extension pattern on this cake consists of traditional drop threadwork alternating with fine dropped loops and piping. Pre-cut extension pieces are used to support the bridgework. There is a delicate balance between the wild rose embroidery which combined with delicate drop loops and piping carries down over the extension work.

The side floral spray is positioned after the completion of the extension detail.

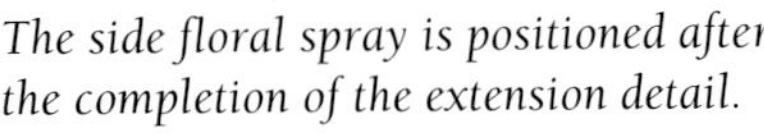

EXTENSION WORK

Mavis Mepham

ractice is the secret of good extension work not necessarily how fine or delicate the work is and there are a few basic techniques that need to be perfected.

Extension work can have the support of a piped on built-out bridge, thin cut-outs of gum paste or float with no support. With bridge support, the edges must be even and smooth so that dropped lines are parallel when looking sideways. If one line is out, it can be seen.

Prepare the cake, cover and place on a covered board. Hide any imperfections on the cake surface by brushing them with royal icing.

Pipe a tiny beading in royal icing around the bottom of the cake where it touches the board. This must be done before proceeding with any decoration. It hides any untidy bits and links the cake to the board. Filigree pieces have been added to this cake and these are described later.

To pipe a support for the extension use a stiff peak royal icing to hold the shape. The extension can be straight or curved up like scallops with a straight top to the bridging lines or curved top and bottom or curved out at the bottom to make the extension look like a frill. There are so many different designs. The hardest decision is to decide which will suit the shape of the cake.

Shown here is a scalloped extension which is flat against the cake. With this the bridge will scallop around the cake but the bottom edge will remain the same distance from the cake. The length of each scallop must be calculated so that there are an even number

The first step in extension work is to pipe a beading around the lower edge to neaten the cake.

around the cake. Mark the top line of the extension work around the cake.

Extension work needs to be kept directly in front of you as you work. As you progress keep turning the cake ever so slightly to stop any tendency to slant the drop lines.

Touch the top marked line and anchor well with a little squeeze, keep an even squeeze until almost to the bottom and stop pressure. Stretch the piped line and wipe the point of the piping tube over the bottom line. If the lines are protruding, smooth out with a damp brush.

The first line of extension piping should touch the cake with no gaps. If there is a flaw in the surface of the cake fill it in first and smooth over. Keep the outer lines level with the first line. Pipe about five or six lines with a no. 2 piping tube, making sure the outer edge has no flaws. Check that there are no gaps or spaces otherwise these will show through as shadows. Brush these spaces with runny royal icing.

Floating extension needs to be supported while it is being piped. The most popular is a line of piping with a no. 1 piping tube which is left in. With true floating work the base or support is taken right away leaving the lines suspended. Dots between the ends are piped to give it security and look nice as an edging.

Whichever way you do it, support your piping hand as you go. After piping for a half-hour, take the icing out of the bag and beat it with the remaining icing in the basin until it has regained its consistency. Place the icing in a clean bag and clean out the piping tube before starting again.

The experienced decorator can embroider over the lines using a soft icing and not let the tip of the pipe touch the extension at the base.

To do open designs, pipe over the dropped work and when it is dry, touch the extension lines behind with a damp, not wet, brush until it is clear with no lines behind.

Finish off the extension work with lace or other decoration of your choice.

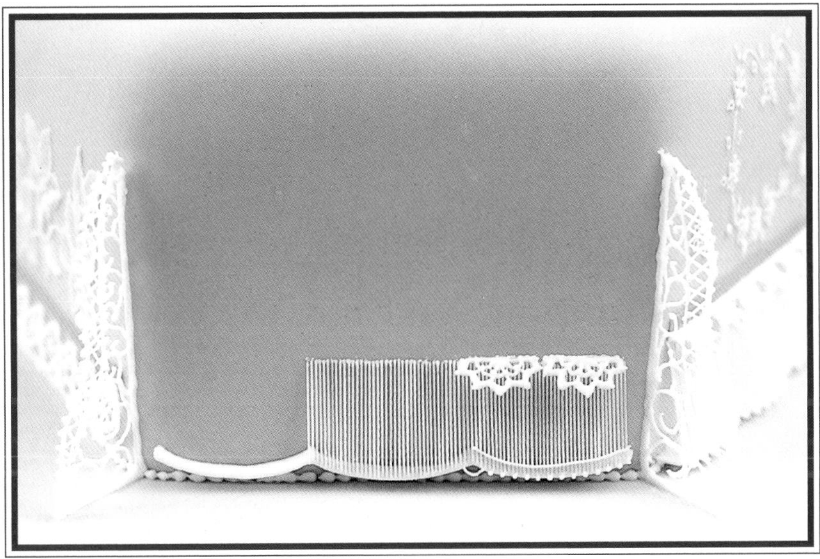

The extension is piped in scallops to support the bridgework.

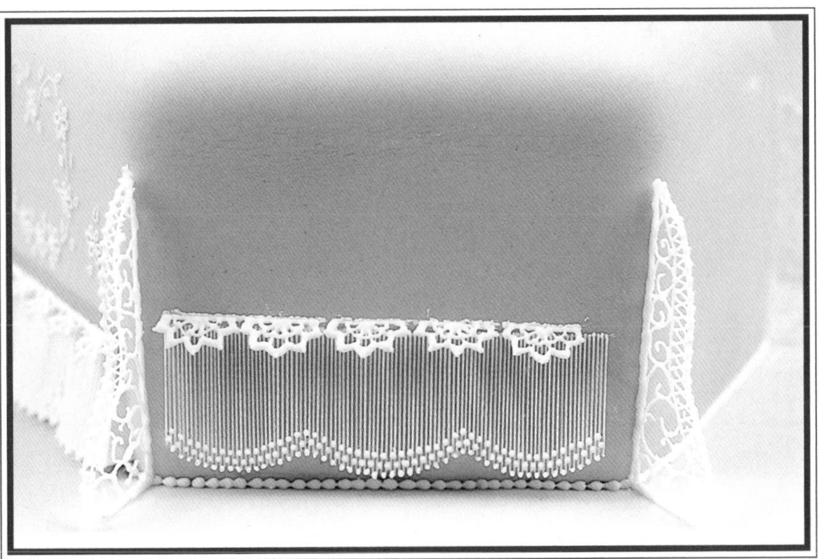

Fine bridgework is finished with lace pieces.

WATERFALL EXTENSION WORK

Kath Swansbra

lthough extension work is established as the finishing touch to the lower edge of almost all show cakes it is seldom used in any other way. It was with this idea in mind that I decided to make use of extension work somewhere else in the design and the waterfall proved the perfect medium.

Perfect planning is necessary so that each part of the design is completed in the right order. There are rocks and flowers tucked in the cave behind the waterfall and these had to be made, dried and coloured first. They are then placed in position and secured.

The waterfall is piped using a very fine piping tube. The drop threadwork is quite long and must extend to the next tier just as water would flow. Support your hand as you go and take your time making sure that there is not too much icing in the bag and that you are positioned directly in front of the area. If your hands are at an angle, the piping lines will not be straight.

After the waterfall is dry, the lichens, mosses and rocks around the water are placed in position with royal icing.

The extension work around the base of each tier is in symmetrical scallops topped with a fine lace edge.

All work on this cake is edible. All the flowers, rocks, etc. are made from sugar according to the schedule for the FHA Salon Culinaire and there are no wires or purchased supports.

Right: An unsupported bridgework waterfall is the main feature of this gold medal prize winner.
(See page 169.)

Opposite: Traditional extension work is the finishing touch on each tier.

LATTICE EXTENSION

Linda McGlinn

his is a variation of the usual straight work. The first row of bridgework is piped vertically and the second is piped at an angle forming a lattice pattern. It is a difficult technique and it is a good idea to plan the pattern carefully.

The longer the vertical lines of the bridge the more difficult they are to achieve. Long lines drag inwards and break easily while being piped. So if you are a bit unsure of your ability, design a lattice with shorter lines. The base or extension must be thoroughly dry before beginning the bridgework. This can take several days. Above all, don't be afraid of a challenge.

Mark the top edge on the cake at the height and shape of your pattern. Build out the base or extension as far as you wish, e.g. five or six rows with a no. 2 piping tube, eight rows with a no. 1 piping tube or fifteen rows with a no. 000 piping tube.

Any of these is suitable and the choice depends on your confidence. The finer the piping tube the greater the degree of difficulty. The rows must be very even with no gaps between each scallop. Allow this base to dry thoroughly over several days.

When the extension is dry begin piping the straight bridgework. Space these lines well apart approximately 6 mm/$^{1}/_{4}$ in and allow them to dry before continuing.

Begin piping the next row at an angle. It does not matter exactly where you start as long as the lines are parallel. Keep the lines as straight as possible. If you wish, neaten the edge of the bridgework with lace or other decoration.

The crossover effect looks wonderful and creates a great deal of interest on the side of any cake. Persistence is the only way to master such a technique.

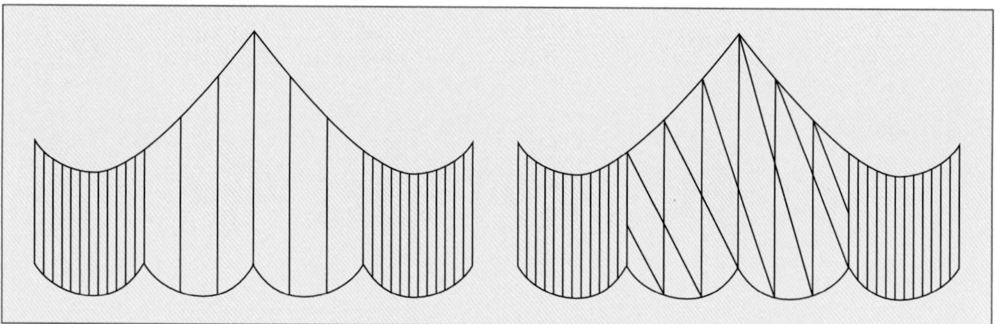
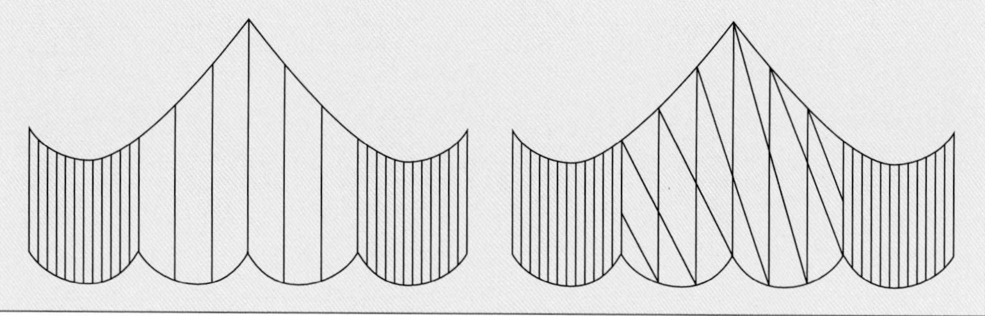

Design for lattice extension.

Opposite: The most important thing in extension work is the ability to pipe straight lines that are perfectly parallel. *(See page 181.)*

STIFFENED RIBBON EXTENSION

Kath Swansbra

his exquisite deep extension work is supported by stiffened ribbon. It is very intricate work but it allows deep scallops of extension work to float off the surface of the cake.

Ice the board on which the cake will stand and allow it to dry out for about a week.

Measure the circumference of the cake and calculate the number of ribbon curves you will place around the cake. Also calculate the depth of the curve of each ribbon and thus the ribbon lengths. Cut these ribbon lengths from satin ribbon 1.25 cm/$\frac{1}{2}$ in wide. Always cut a few extra lengths.

Choose a container that is approximately the curve you have chosen for the ribbon. A small rolling pin, spice jars or even cotton reels are ideal choices. Cover the container with non-stick transparent paper or baking paper.

To make the sugar syrup, boil $\frac{1}{2}$ cup/125 mL/4 fl oz water, $\frac{1}{2}$ cup/125 g/4 oz sugar and $1\frac{1}{2}$ teaspoons of glucose together for five minutes. Store in the refrigerator in a glass jar.

Lightly brush each strip of ribbon with the sugar syrup. Place the strips over the curved container and stick down each end with tape. Make sure each strip is straight and allow to dry overnight.

Cover the entire iced board with wax paper. Place the uniced cake in the correct position on the board and cover with icing. Be careful not to damage the icing on the board through the wax paper. Cut away any excess wax paper and pipe a small beading around the cake base. Leave aside to dry.

Mark the desired height line for the straight ribbon around the cake and also mark the position of the stiffened ribbon pieces around the base of the cake. Use a scalpel to cut slits at the required height above the base of cake. Insert the ends of each stiffened ribbon length in each slit. Continue around the circumference of the cake and allow to set. When the icing on the cake is dry attach the straight ribbon on the ribbon line.

Pipe the bridge lines from underneath the straight ribbon line to the extended ribbon at the base. Use a small damp brush to keep the ribbon extension clean from any excess royal icing. Using royal icing, stick a ribbon strip vertically from the straight ribbon line down the side of the cake to fit between the joins in the ribbon extension. Attach lace at the top of the bridgework.

Design for ribbon extension.

The cream ribbon loops are stiffened with sugar syrup before being positioned. *(See page 173.)*

FLANNEL FLOWER EXTENSION WORK

Eileen Scriven

he side design on this cake is made in two sections to incorporate two different methods. The upper section features Australian native flannel flowers piped on pieces of tulle and suspended between triangular-shaped pieces of moulding paste which are finished with narrow ribbon. The same narrow ribbon runs around the circumference of the built-out pieces and the bridge is floated between that and the board.

Prepare the fondant board and leave to dry thoroughly. When dry place the cake in position and cover. Measure the circumference of the cake and then calculate the number and size of the tulle pieces required. Trace your flower pattern onto non-stick paper. You will need a pattern for each piece of tulle. Cut out the tulle pieces and lay out on the non-stick paper. Pipe the flowers onto the tulle carefully following the pattern underneath. Do a few extras.

Cut the required number of moulding paste triangles needed between each piece of tulle. Mark the position line of the top piece of straight ribbon on the cake. Then mark the lower line. Mark the position of the triangles.

Attach the triangles using a little royal icing and make sure they are straight. Place the top ribbon in position and attach each piece of embroidered tulle to the top ribbon and triangles. Cut the required number of ribbon lengths needed to go between each piece of tulle. These pieces run to the bottom of the piped extension work.

Pipe a bridge to support the extension and place the vertical ribbon lengths in position between each piece of tulle and over the triangles. Attach a second straight ribbon around the cake at the base of the tulle flower pieces.

Using a no. 00 piping tube, pipe the extension between the lower ribbon and the bridge. Place tiny ribbon knots at the end of each vertical ribbon.

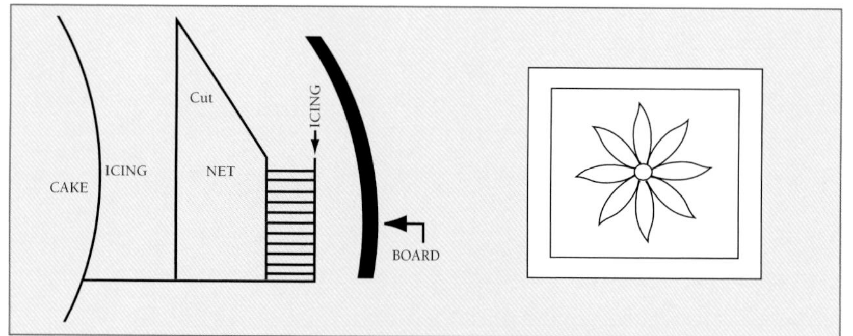

Overhead plan of extension work and pattern for flannel flower.

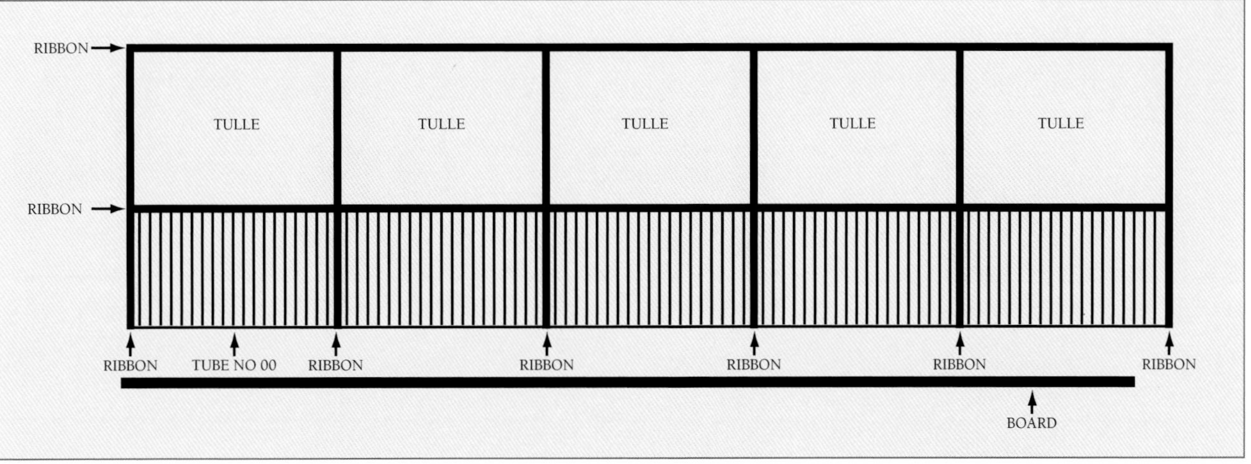

Side plan for extension work.

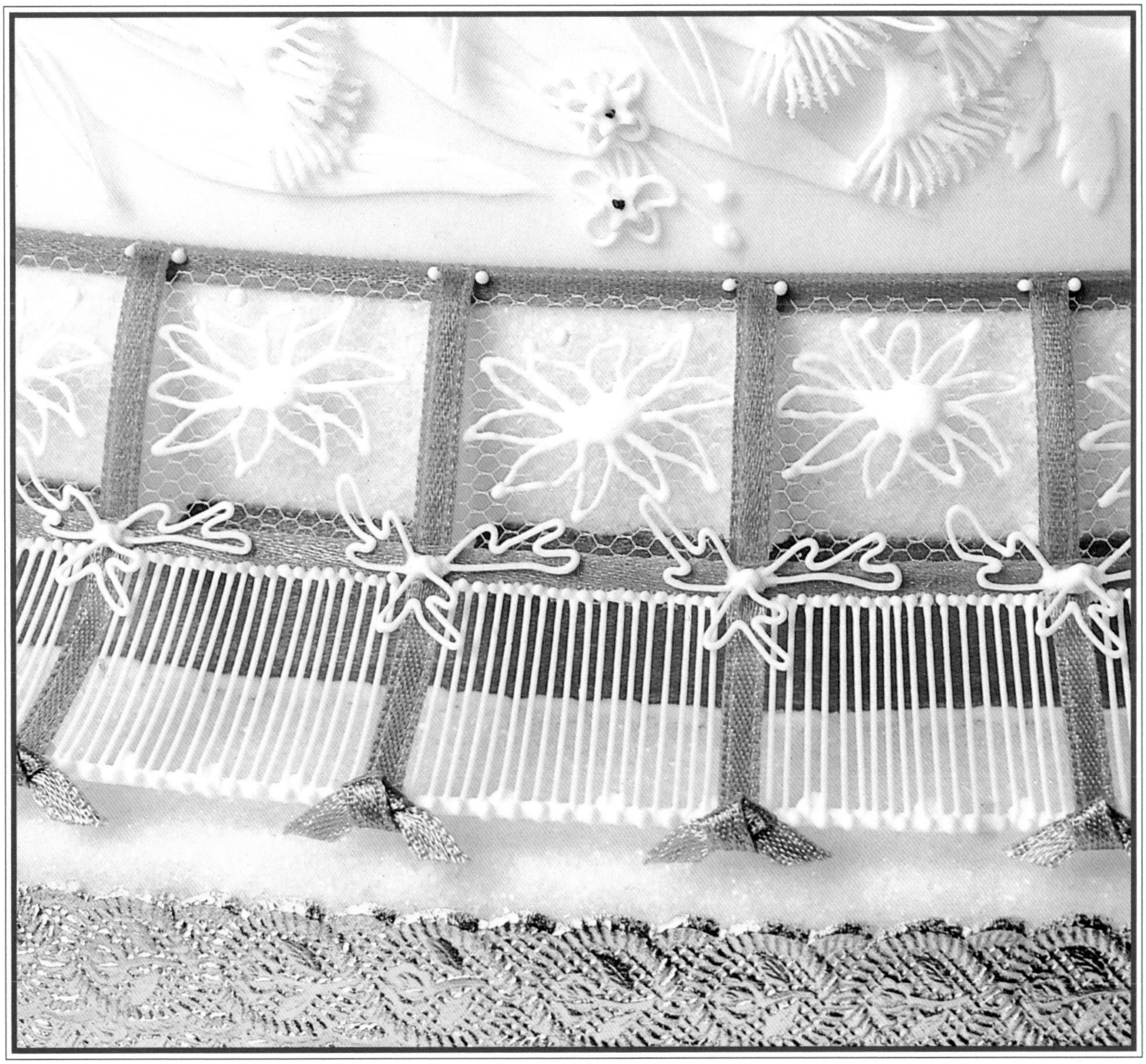

Each flannel flower is piped on cotton tulle and suspended between ribbon. (See page 185.)

HANDKERCHIEF LACE EXTENSION

Dorothy Allison

fter having mastered conventional bridgework it is great to develop a new idea which makes use of the same skills but opens the door to many variations. Handkerchief lace extension is a fresh, relatively simple option to the floating bridgework method.

Draw up a design for the side of the cake and determine the height of the bridgework and the size of the scallop. Transfer this pattern to the sides of the cake using pin pricks.

Using a no. 0 piping tube and royal icing, pipe a series of neat, small dots evenly spaced around the lower guideline. Allow a little time for these foundation dots to dry.

Using the same piping tube, repeat this process building the next layer of dots onto the foundation dots. Allow time for this second layer to dry. Repeat this process until there are four or five layers of dots, depending on the angle at which you wish your bridgework to extend from the side.

Using a no. 00 piping tube, join the dots with uniform scallops and allow to dry before proceeding.

Using a no. 00 piping tube (or a no. 000 or smaller for those who enjoy a challenge) and an icing bag made from florist's cellophane, pipe the bridgework and smooth out with a fine damp brush.

To finish apply fine dots to the lower edge of the bridgework to camouflage the scallop.

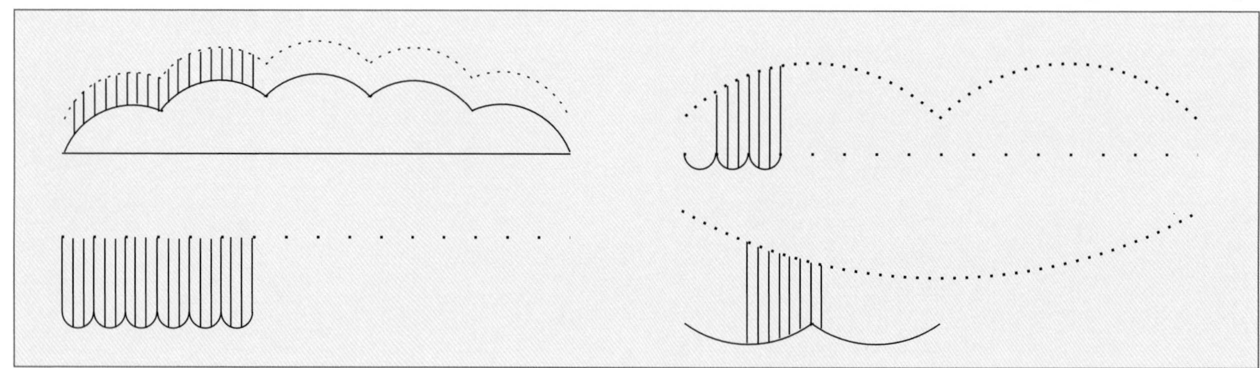

Pattern for handkerchief lace extension.

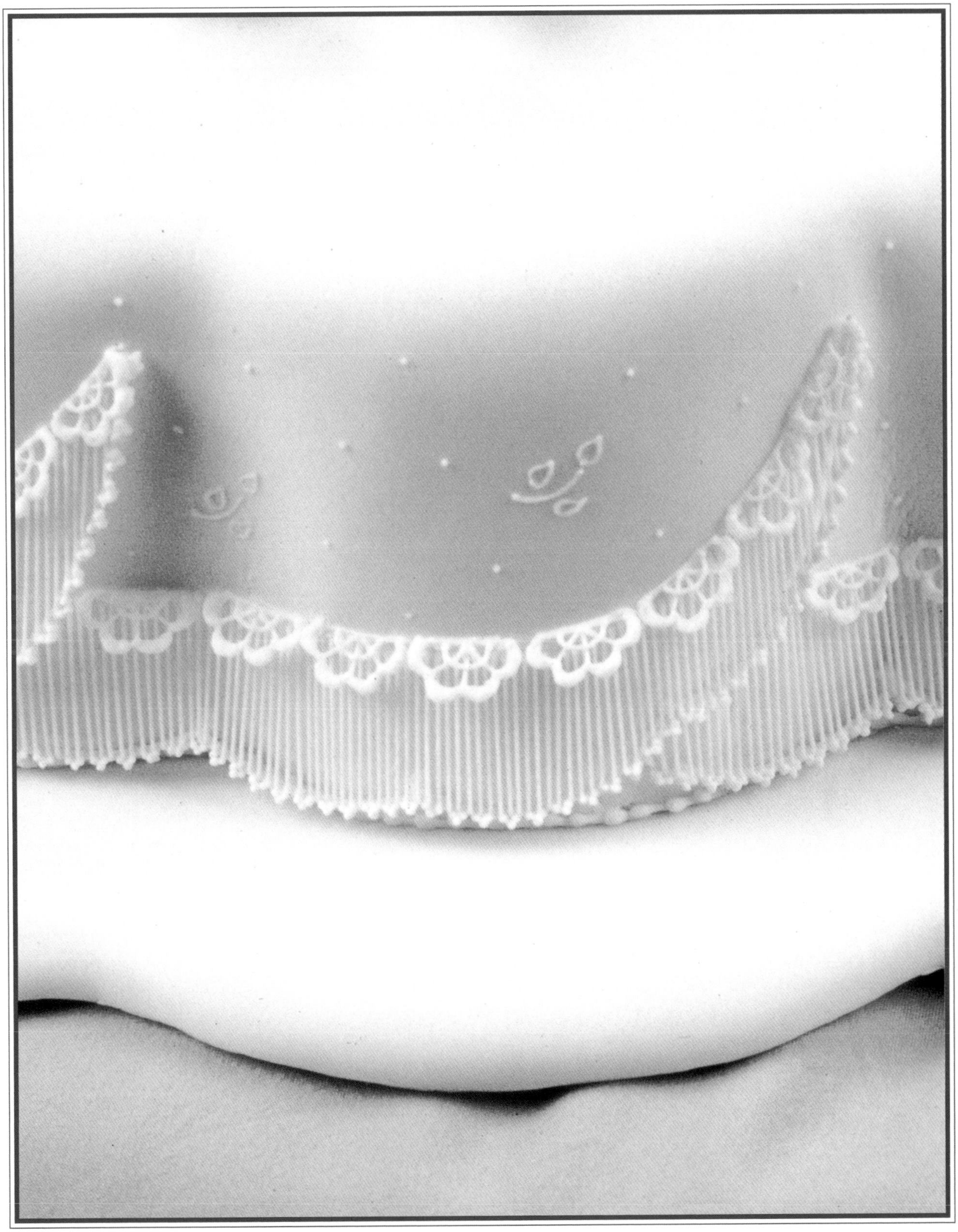

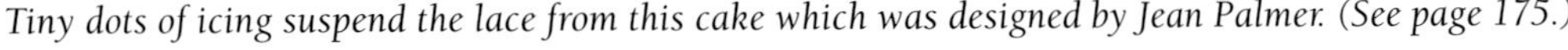

Tiny dots of icing suspend the lace from this cake which was designed by Jean Palmer. *(See page 175.)*

SECTION THREE

VARIOUS TECHNIQUES

SUGAR PULLING

MARZIPAN

SCULPTURE

Ribbons • Animals • Novelty
Figurines

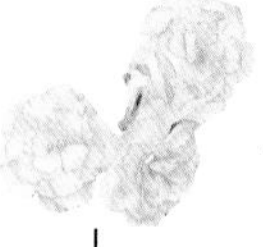

SUGAR RIBBONS

Hervé Boutin

These dazzling ribbons are all made using pulled sugar. A sugar syrup is made and coloured in batches then the different coloured batches are combined and stretched to form ribbons. The secret of course is practice.

To make a good sugar syrup boil together 4 cups/1 kg/2 lb sugar, 1½ cups/375 mL/12 fl oz water, ¾ cup/185 mL/6 fl oz liquid glucose. For pulled sugar a few drops of tartaric acid solution or lemon juice are added to give softness to the sugar when pulling.

Use a strong copper saucepan if possible. Put the water into the saucepan then add the sugar and mix thoroughly either with a whisk or a large spoon. This helps dissolve the sugar. Gradually heat the syrup until it boils and add the glucose and stir using a wooden spoon. As the syrup boils a scum will form on top. This must be removed with a wet brush. Also, clean up the sides of the saucepan to remove any undissolved sugar. A lid can be placed on the top of the saucepan for thirty seconds and the steam will automatically clean up the sides and remove any crystals.

The sugar should be cooked as quickly as possible otherwise the syrup may turn yellow which is a problem if a white or blue colour is wanted.

Ten drops of tartaric acid or lemon juice should be added while the sugar is boiling at 130°C/260°F to 135°C/275°F when cooking sugar syrup for pulling.

To check if the sugar is cooked drop a little in cold water. The sugar droplet must crack and turn hard immediately. A candy thermometer can also be used. The correct temperature is somewhere between 155°C/310°F to 160°C/320°F.

Divide the toffee into batches and add the colour. Pour the mixture onto a lightly oiled marble slab or silicon mat. Pull the sugar until it has a good shine. It should not be pulled too hard or it will crystallise and turn milky.

Use small amounts of each colour and roll out to form a thin sausage. Lay each colour side by side and pull the whole thing. Treat it gently and it will maintain its gloss. The bows are twisted and attached to the ribbon ends by melting the join over a heat lamp. All the batches must be at the same temperature before combining to pull a ribbon.

Opposite and this page: Different coloured batches of cooked syrup are pulled to form exquisite satin ribbons.

SUGAR FRUITS

Hervé Boutin

ruits add an exotic touch to desserts and are often used to decorate them. These fruits have been formed from boiled sugar syrup placed on a sugar pump and blown into shape. The technique is very similar to glass blowing.

Make a sugar syrup by boiling together 4 cups/1 kg/2 lb sugar, 1½ cups/375 mL/12 fl oz water and ¾ cup/185 mL/6 fl oz glucose.

Put the water into a copper saucepan then add the sugar and mix thoroughly with a whisk or a large spoon to help dissolve the sugar. Gradually heat the syrup until it boils. Add the glucose and stir using a wooden spoon. Use a wet brush to remove any scum that forms on top. Clean up the sides of the saucepan to remove any undissolved sugar. The sugar should be cooked as quickly as possible otherwise the syrup may turn yellow which is a problem if a white or blue colour is wanted.

To check if the sugar is cooked drop a little in cold water. The sugar droplet must crack and turn hard immediately. A candy thermometer can also be used. The correct temperature is between 155°C/310°F to 160°C/320°F. When cooked the mixture should be poured onto a lightly oiled marble slab or silicone sheet and pulled gently to create shine. Be gentle or the mixture will go milky.

Place 60g/2 oz of sugar mixture on a sugar pump and blow to the right shape. Obviously, this is a task that takes practice. Spray or paint the fruit in the desired colours.

Peaches and apricots must be gently rolled in cornflour/cornstarch to create the skin texture which characterises these fruits.

Opposite and this page: Just like glass blowing, these beautiful fruits are shaped by blowing cooked syrup on a sugar pump.

SUGAR BIRDS

Hervé Boutin

lways a symbol of love, and peace, these magnificent birds create a romantic setting on any table. They have been made using three main techniques, sugar blowing, sugar pulling and sugar pouring.

The hearts and the other bases have been made with poured sugar using a frame. These frames can be existing metal tins or trays or alternately you can make your own shape using children's play dough or plasticine. The frame should be very lightly sprayed with oil before pouring in the syrup.

The cloudy appearance is obtained by adding two teaspoons of calcium carbonate mixed to a paste. This is enough for 4 cups/1 kg/2 lb sugar. This is added to the syrup at about 130°C/260°F. After the addition of the calcium carbonate continue boiling the syrup until it reaches the hard crack stage.

Opposite and this page: Three advanced sugar techniques are used to make these centrepieces. The bases are poured, the ribbons are pulled and the bird shapes are formed on a sugar pump.

Remove the syrup from the heat and pour onto an oiled marble slab or silicone paper and gently pull to bring out the shine. Place about 250 g/8 oz of sugar mixture on a sugar pump and blow until the desired shape is formed. The wings can be pulled into shape. The eyes are painted with a fine brush or you can make a marzipan eye. The ribbons are made using the pulled sugar method. The whole creations are assembled by gently heating the joins over a spirit lamp and setting in place.

Opposite and this page: Hours and hours of practice are the only way to master the art of forming such elegant swans, doves and ribbons.

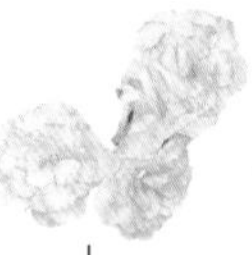

CORNUCOPIA

Hervé Boutin

obody seems quite sure where this type of centrepiece originated. However it is always seen as one depicting a richness of fare. The horn here is made from blown and pulled sugar and the miniature fruits are made from marzipan.

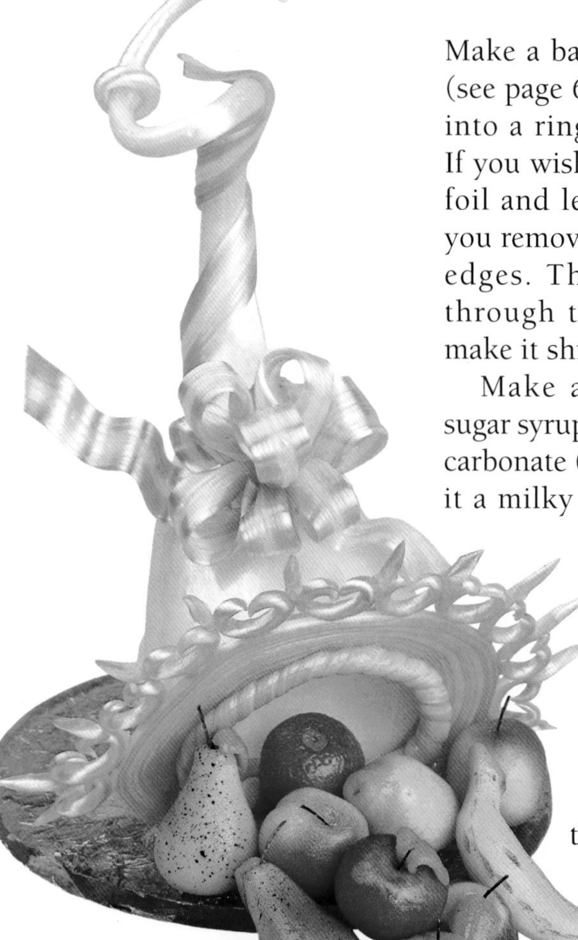

Make a batch of sugar syrup, (see page 61) colour and pour into a ring to form the base. If you wish, line the ring with foil and leave in place when you remove the base. Trim the edges. The foil will reflect through the sugar base and make it shimmer.

Make a second batch of sugar syrup containing calcium carbonate (see page 62) to give it a milky appearance. When cooked, gently pull it into a bright shine then place about 250 g/8 oz of sugar mixture on a sugar pump and blow until the desired shape for the horn is achieved. Colour a second batch of syrup in a pale pink and pull to form the collar. Twist two sections of pink to form the rope which is used to finish off the opening.

The ribbon is made from two batches of syrup, white and pink. Twist the ribbon into an extravagant bow and attach to the horn by melting a little over a spirit lamp and placing immediately in position.

Prepare a batch of marzipan and shape into miniature fruit shapes. The leaves are made separately. Colour the fruits with good quality concentrated colour. Allow to dry and then attach the leaves. Paint in the details of the skin markings on the fruit using a fine brush.

Melt a small patch underneath the horn and attach immediately to the base. Place the centrepiece in position and arrange the marzipan fruits so that they flow over the table. Fabulous.

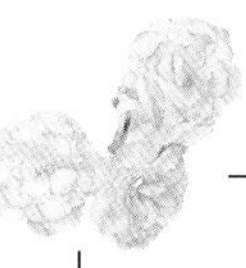

EASTER BUNNY

Hervé Boutin

his very quizzical Easter bunny is made from poured sugar and is very easy to make. He is a great attention grabber at any party. Any type of creature can be made this way, particularly Santa or a favourite cartoon character.

First draw or trace the pattern for the whole piece. Next trace this a few more times. These are used to make the arms, feet, ears and all the other extra bits. Decide which parts are to be poured or coloured separately.

Prepare a batch of syrup (see page 61) and pour into a round mould for the base. Set aside. Prepare a board that is large enough for the main piece. Place the pattern on the board. Form children's play dough or plasticine around the edge of the pattern. Neaten the dough so that the edge of the bunny will be smooth. Lightly oil the pattern.

Make a batch of syrup (see page 61) and colour to your taste. Pull gently to bring out the shine and then pour into the mould. Leave to set.

Cut out the other parts of the bunny from the extra tracings and keep all the one colour together. Use play dough or plasticine to form the outline for all the parts in the next colour on the body.

Each panel and colour on this quizzical rabbit is poured in a mould. The trim is piped on later and he is supported by a triangle of toffee.

Make a batch of syrup (see page 61) colour and pull, then pour into the sections of the main body.

Continue in this manner, pouring the different colours on top of each other until you have finished your creation. Carefully remove from the moulds and neaten the edges.

The Easter eggs and necktie are made separately and joined on later. Make a triangle to support the bunny on the base. Melt one edge of the triangle and place in position on the base. Melt the upright edge of the triangle and place the Easter bunny in position.

Use royal icing to pipe on his facial features and to outline his ears and necktie. Arrange Easter eggs around the base if you like.

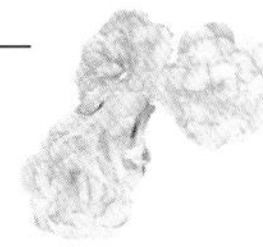

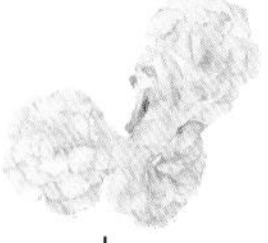
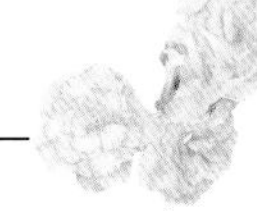

CORAL FANTASY

Hervé Boutin

oral Fantasy is a colourful presentation which combines four different sugar techniques—poured, bubble, pulled and blown sugar. Each is a variation on a batch of sugar syrup.

For the flat pieces the various colours have been poured in different rings and shapes and then assembled using a base of caramel.

Bubble sugar is an interesting technique. Lay a sheet of non-stick paper or silicone on a flat surface and use a paint brush to splatter a little alcohol on the paper. As soon as the sugar is cooked and coloured pour it onto the paper. The heat causes the alcohol to evaporate and create bubbles in the syrup. These create wonderful reflection of light and give a fantastic underwater appearance.

The fish is formed from blown sugar. Form 60 g/2 oz cooked sugar syrup on a sugar pump and blow to the desired shape.

The ribbons are formed with pulled sugar and twisted into shape.

When all the pieces are cold, it is time for assembly. Take your time and try the different parts in position before sticking them. The final positioning depends on how your individual pieces are shaped.

Use an air brush and paint brush to bring out the soft colours of the coral.

The shimmering coral is made by pouring cooked syrup over paper that has been sprayed with alcohol.

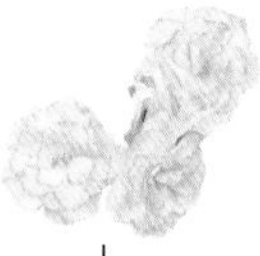
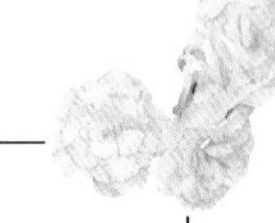

COBBERS

Linda McGlinn

his icing sculpture depicts a typical scene of the Australian outback early this century. Cobber is an old-fashioned term for a friend or mate and is seldom used now. The man in this sculpture is called a swagman—a drifter who carried all his belongings in a swag or roll on his back. A swaggie usually wore a hat with corks hanging from the brim to keep the bush flies from his face. He was often accompanied by his dog. The bread he is feeding his dog is called damper which is a simple dough cooked in either a covered container or camp oven over an open fire or just straight in the ashes. It was usually eaten with golden syrup.

This turn-of-the-century Australian bush scene is made from moulding paste which is then formed into shape and painted.

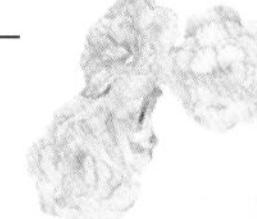

Detailed hand painting is the secret of this magnificent sculpture.

The most difficult thing in producing a work such as this is keeping the correct proportions. Draw or trace the whole picture and then reduce or enlarge it to fit. From this determine the size of the individual elements and sketch or trace a pattern of these.

Prepare the base board and then cover with dirt and grit made from moulding paste passed through a sieve or just crumbled. If desired the log can be made from cake covered with royal icing and painted. Alternatively the whole thing can be formed on a base of styrofoam.

Opposite and this page: Every detail of this piece is authentic in colour and detail. A work such as this is the result of years of experience.

The construction of the swagman is done in moulding paste. Form the torso and dress it in shirt, waistcoat and tie. The collar can be added later to hide the join on the neck. Add the legs with trousers on, then place the jacket on the body so that it hangs over the legs a little. Add the arms with the sleeves attached and finally the hands and the feet. The head and face are hand moulded. Finally add the hair and the hat and arrange him in the final position on the log.

The dog is made from moulding paste with his front paws added last.

The swag or roll is simply made from a roll of moulding paste. The damper is a ball of moulding paste with a wedge removed. The final effects of crumbling bread, etc. are achieved by experimentation.

After assembly of the main objects, add the detail such as an old can, rocks and other bits and pieces.

The look and feel of a piece such as this can only be achieved by the final painting and colouring. Take your time and use a good quality brush. Mix enough of each colour to complete the area as it is almost impossible to match colour later on. The final result will be a piece to treasure for years to come.

WILD BIRD

Gail Gambrell

aught just before takeoff this bird somehow resembles a dove of peace. The whole piece is made from pastillage paste and hand coloured after assembly.

BODY

Shape the body as shown in the pattern. The body is 7.5 cm/3 in long and 2.5 cm/1 in wide. If you adjust the body size all the other pieces must be adjusted accordingly including the feathers.

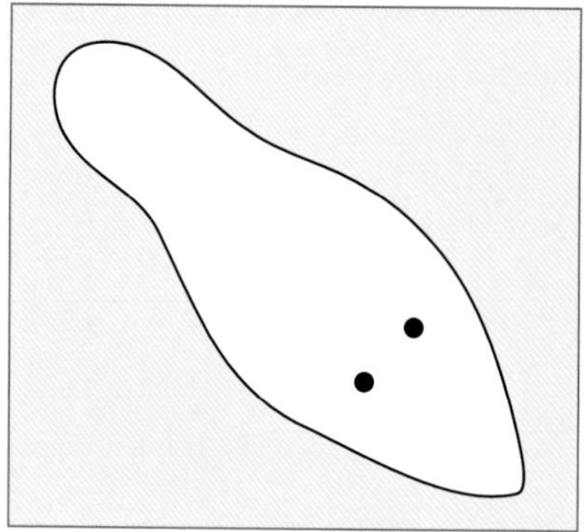

Pattern for body showing leg positions.

LEGS

To strengthen the legs, push two lengths of dry spaghetti into the belly of the bird's body towards the tail end. Place the body upside down in soft wadding or cotton wool and allow to dry thoroughly.

WINGS

Determine the length of the finished bird's wings and then make two small wings one-third of the total length of the finished wing. Brush a small amount of gum glue at the base of the wings and attach to the top of the bird's body closer to the head than the tail. Place the whole piece into wadding or cotton wool with the legs down and allow to dry thoroughly before proceeding.

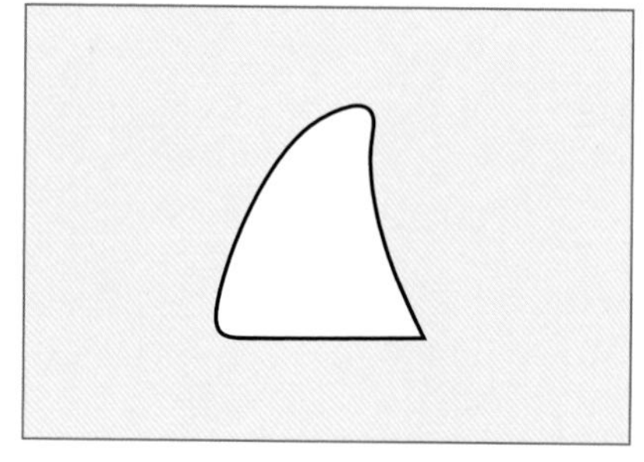

Pattern for wing.

FEATHER VEINER

Cut small lengths of fine wire and glue on a firm surface as shown on the pattern.

Feather veiner.

FEATHERS

You need to make a number of large feathers for the tail and wings, medium and small feathers for the wings and tiny feathers for the body.

Tail

Take a ball of lavender-coloured pastillage paste and roll out very thinly. Cut ten large feathers. Place each feather down the centre of the veiner and press gently. Place each feather onto soft foam and ball the edges slightly. Lay the feathers flat to dry.

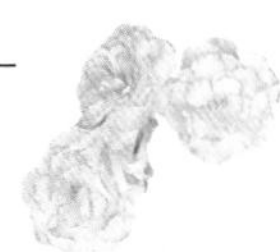

Each feather is hand cut and veined before being placed in position.

Feather placed on veiner.

Colour each feather orange at the top, brown in the centre and lavender on the end.

First Layer

Attach four feathers to the tail end using royal icing.

Second Layer

Alternate three feathers over the top of the first layer.

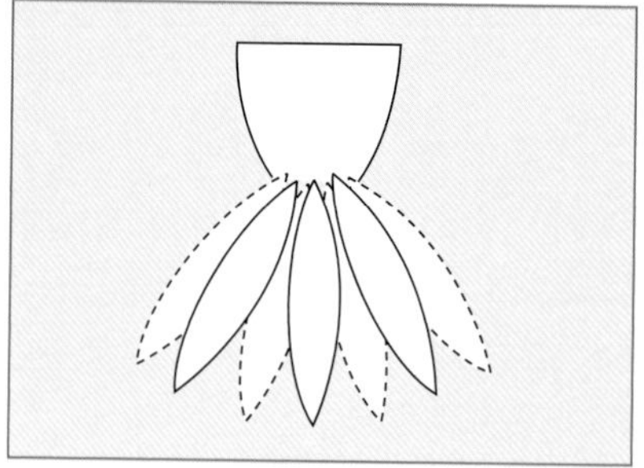

First and second layers of feathers.

Last Layers

Lay two feathers on top of the second layer and then one feather on top to finish.

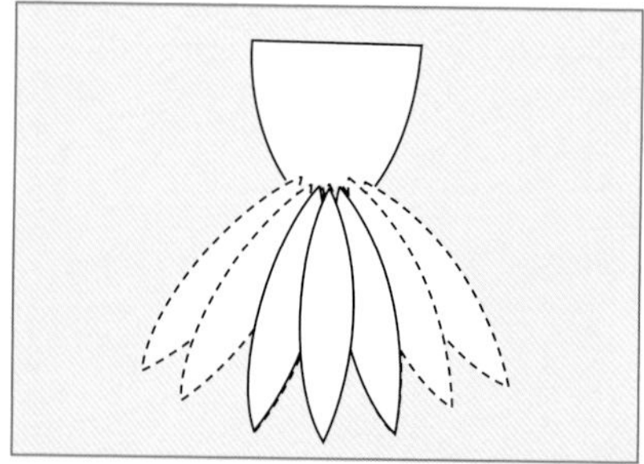

Last layers of feathers.

WINGS

Cut out six large feathers, six medium feathers and six small feathers. There is a set of three for each wing. Vein the feathers, allow to dry and then colour them the same as the tail feathers.

Attach three large feathers to the wing tip, layering from the top down. Then attach three medium feathers layering from the large feathers down. Attach three small feathers to the wing edge, layering from the medium feathers down to finish the wing edge.

Arrangement of wing feathers.

Cut a large number of small feathers and vein. Keep them covered so they don't dry out. Attach feathers to the upper side of the wing while soft, layering from the front edge to the base of the wing. Completely cover the wing and continue to make a few layers. Repeat for underneath the wing then repeat the whole process for the other wing.

Place two rows of these small feathers around the base of the tail covering over where the tail feathers are attached.

BODY FEATHERS

Use a small daphne cutter to cut the body feathers. Separate the petals from the shape with a scalpel. The petals will be used as feathers. Vein each petal/feather and cover so they don't dry out. Finish covering the bird's body with these tiny feathers layering from the base of the bird to its head. When dry, dust with lavender chalk.

BEAK

Using a 5 cm/2 in ball of brown pastillage paste, make a cone shape. Flatten slightly and cut through one end using fine sharp scissors. Attach to the bird's face with royal icing.

EYES

Form two tiny balls of black pastillage paste and attach to either side of the bird's head with gum glue. Place a tiny dot of white royal icing onto each eye to give highlights.

LEGS

Wrap pale brown pastillage paste around the spaghetti to form the bird's legs.

FINISH

Place the bird onto an icing log. Pipe three pale brown toes in front of the bird's legs where they attach to the log.

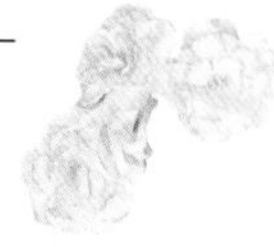

The log and flowers are made from pastillage paste and hand painted.

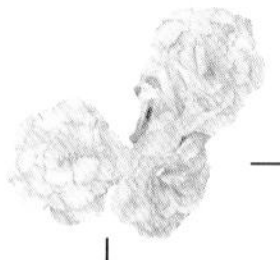

TURTLE

Gail Gambrell

here is nothing more appealing than a man who's sure of himself and here we have a cool guy with ego and attitude. And to top it off he's cute.

SHELL MOULD

Using a hard drying moulding paste, make a mould to form the turtle's shell. The turtle mould is 7.5 cm/3 in long x 5 cm/2 in wide tapering to 9 cm/3½ in long x 6.5 cm/2½ in wide and curved. Using a knife, make cuts about 8 mm/⅓ in deep across the top of the mould. If you wish, a small oval dish can be used instead. It is easier than making one freehand.

Pattern for shell base.

SHELL BASE

Turn the shell mould upside down. Measure the mould and cut an oval paper pattern large enough to fit around the base of the mould. Roll out a piece of pale brown pastillage paste 3 mm/⅛ in thick. Cut an oval icing piece using the paper pattern. Ease the icing oval over the shell mould and leave overnight to dry.

When dry, press small odd-shaped pieces of pastillage paste around the outside edge of the shell, leaving a space between each piece. Brush around the top edge of the shell with gum glue. Form a long 3 mm/⅛ in thick sausage roll of pastillage paste. Press this down around the top edge of the shell to finish off.

SHELL TOP

Measure the top of the shell mould and cut an oval paper pattern large enough to fit over the mould. Cut 1.25 cm/½ in off each end. Roll out a piece of pale brown pastillage paste to 1.5 mm/1/16 in thick. Using the pattern, cut out an icing oval. Place the pastillage oval over the top of the mould and carefully ease the paste into the grooves. Leave overnight to dry before colouring.

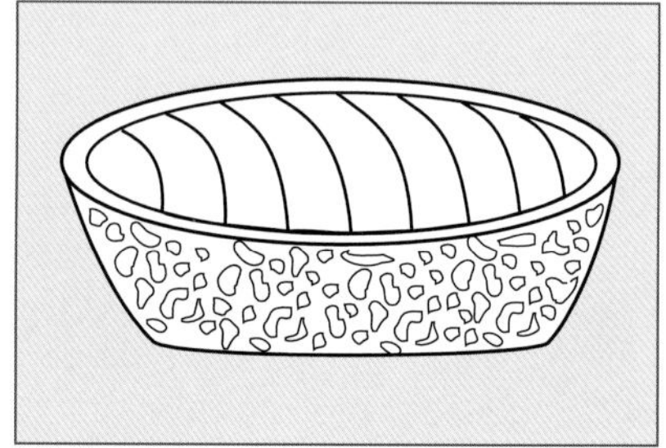

Pattern for completed shell.

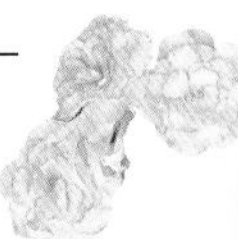

COLOURING SHELLS

Use dark green, light green, brown and orange chalks and brush the colours in a patchy fashion around the outside of the shell. The base shell should be a brownish shade while the top is greener.

TURTLE NECK

Make a batch of pastillage paste and colour it moss green—green with a touch of brown. Wrap the coloured paste around a small peppermint stick or use four pieces of dry spaghetti each about 5 cm/2 in long. Set aside and allow to dry.

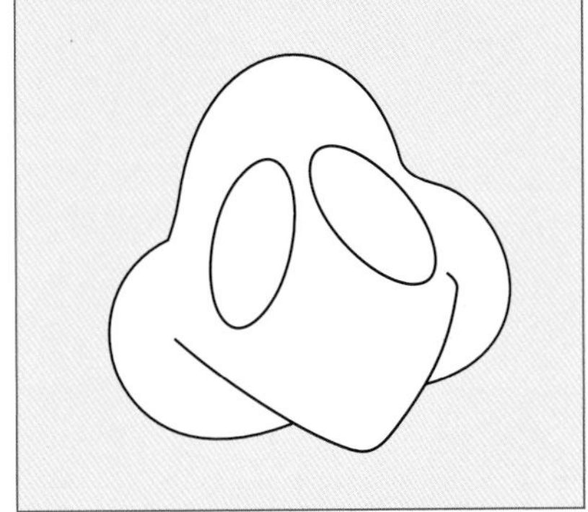

Pattern for face.

TURTLE HEAD

Take a 4.5 cm/$1^{3}/_{4}$ in ball of pastillage paste and make an egg shape. Pull out one side, towards the base, to form a point. Cut a slit across the point to form the turtle beak. Ball out two ovals above the beak to form the eye sockets. Using two 8 mm/$^{1}/_{3}$ in balls of pastillage paste form two oval shapes and press into the balled sockets. Leave slightly raised at the front; don't flatten the eyes on the turtle's face.

The appeal of this piece of sugar art is keeping a cartoon-like feel to the structure.

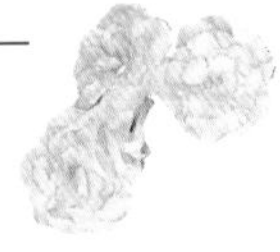

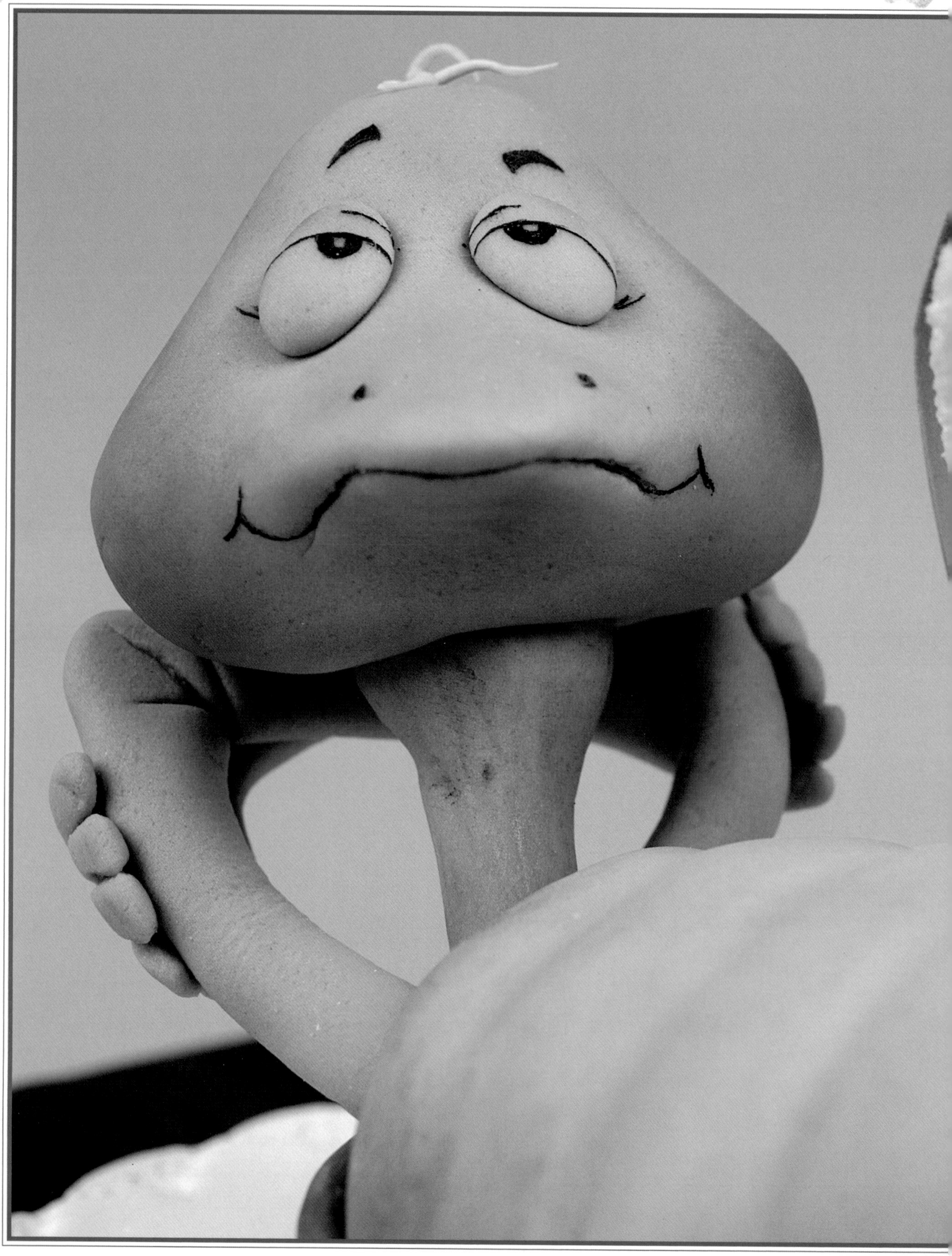

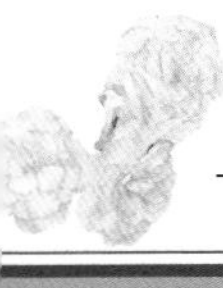
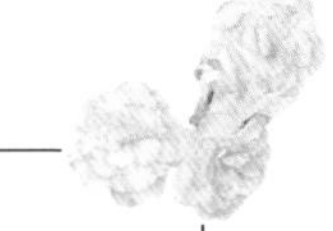

Brush one end of the dried turtle's neck with gum glue. Push the dried neck up into the base of the head. Place aside and allow to dry. When dry, draw on facial expressions using a cake decorating pen.

LEGS

Make a sausage shape 10 cm/4 in long x 8 mm/$^1/_3$ in thick. Leave an oval shape at one end 1.25 cm/$^1/_2$ in long. Flatten the oval to form a foot and cut four slits to form the toes. Press down slightly on the end of each toe to form the toe nails. Push the foot up so it is at right angles to the leg and ease out some of the paste behind where the foot meets the leg to form an ankle. Bend the leg in the centre and ease a small amount of paste out at the front to form a knobbly knee. Make another leg to match. Set aside on foam and allow to dry.

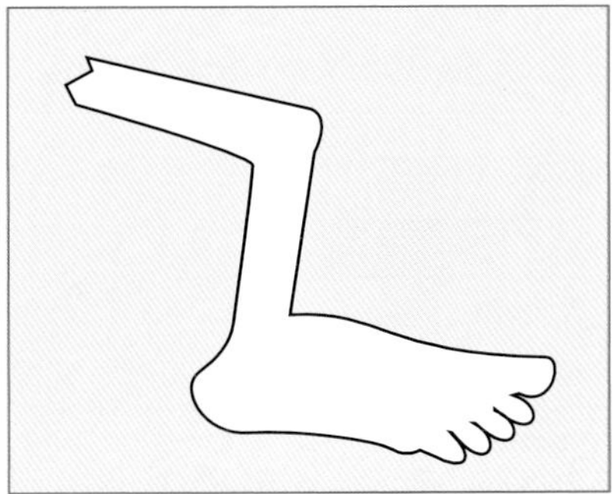

Pattern for leg and foot.

ARMS

Make a sausage shape 10 cm/4 in x 8 mm/$^1/_3$ in thick and leave an oval at one end 1.25 cm/$^1/_2$ in long. Flatten the oval to form a hand. Cut four slits to form the fingers. Press down slightly on each finger to form a finger nail. Bend the arm in half and ease out a small amount of paste on the bend to form a knobbly elbow. Make another arm the same. Set aside and allow to dry.

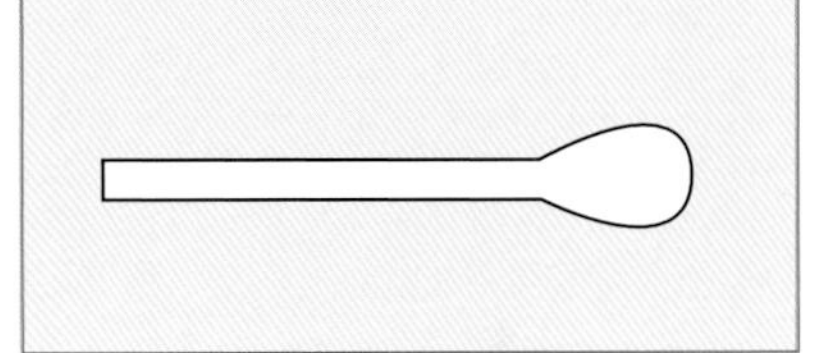

Pattern for arm.

ASSEMBLY

Fill the whole shell base with green pastillage paste. Push the turtle's neck into one end of the shell base. Push the arm ends into the paste on either side of the turtle's neck. Attach the hands to the back of the turtle's head with royal icing. Push the leg into the other end of the shell base. Place the other leg over the first leg.

Roll out some pastillage paste and make the sign. Finish off with grass and flowers.

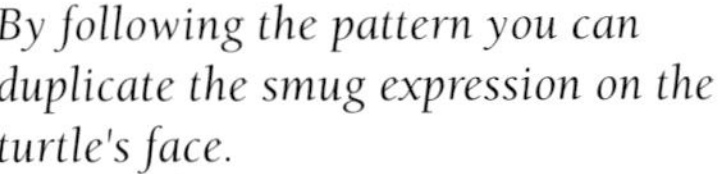

By following the pattern you can duplicate the smug expression on the turtle's face.

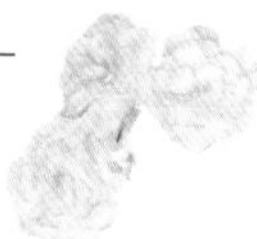

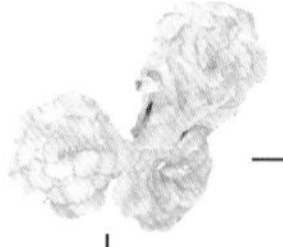

SCULPTURED ELEPHANT

Gail Gambrell

his sleepy elephant is made by gradually building up each element on the body using pastillage paste. Let your own creativity decide the exact position of each piece and your elephant will have his own charm.

BODY AND HEAD

To make the body, use a 5 cm/2 in ball of pale grey pastillage paste and form an oval. Stand it on one end and tilt back.

The head is made using a 3 cm/$1\frac{1}{4}$ in ball of pale grey pastillage paste formed into an oval shape. Lie it on one side in front of the body. Form two 2 cm/$\frac{3}{4}$ in balls of pastillage paste for the cheeks. Place in front of the head, slightly apart.

Very lightly moisten all the pieces. Roll out a 5 cm/2 in ball of pale grey pastillage paste about 2 mm/$\frac{1}{8}$ in thick. Fit over all the pieces and trim neatly to form the body, just like covering a cake.

Using a balling tool, make two slight oval indents just above the cheeks. These are the eye sockets. Make two small oval shapes from pale grey pastillage paste. They should be large enough to protrude slightly. Lightly moisten the eye sockets and place the oval pieces of paste into the indents.

LEGS

Divide a 5 cm/2 in ball of pale grey paste into four pieces. Take two pieces for the front legs and form cone shapes each 5 cm/2 in long. Moisten down one side of each piece and place on either side of the elephant with the wide end at the front level with the cheeks. Using a balling tool, make three indents in the end of each leg for toe nails. Using the blunt side of a scalpel, mark each leg to form knee marks.

Use the other two pieces to form two cones identical to the front legs and curve over your finger. This gives the back legs their curled up appearance. Moisten one side of each leg and attach to the elephant's rear with the narrow part facing the centre of the back. The legs should be curved backwards. Using a balling tool make three indents in each leg for toe nails. Using the blunt side of a scalpel, mark creases to form the elephant's knees.

TRUNK

Use a 2.5 cm/1 in ball of pale grey pastillage paste to form a 5 cm/2 in long sausage shape. Taper each end and hollow out one end using a balling tool. Dampen the other end and attach between the elephant's cheeks then curve the trunk. Using the blunt side of a scalpel mark along the top of the trunk.

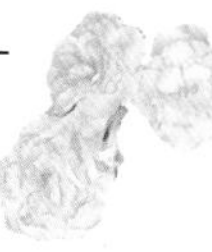

EARS

Take two 2.5 cm/1 in balls of pastillage paste and form two oval shapes. Hold each sideways and thin the outer edge with your fingers, leaving a thicker section where you are holding it. One end of the ear should end up wider than the other—a shape much like your own ear. Moisten along the thick section and attach to the elephant's head. The narrow section of the ear should rest on the elephant's leg. Repeat for the other ear.

TAIL

Make a very thin short sausage shape 1.25 cm/$^{1}/_{2}$ in long for the tail. Attach to the elephant's rear with a small amount of moisture. Pipe three eye lashes at the bottom of each eye using black royal icing. Pipe hair onto the elephant's head between the two ears.

FINISH

Brush a little moisture into each indent in the elephant's feet. Take tiny balls of dark grey pastillage paste and push one into each of the indents to form the toe nails.

Brush the elephant's cheeks, inner ears, eyes and rear with pink chalk to give highlights. Finish the design with a few miniature chocolate bottles if you wish.

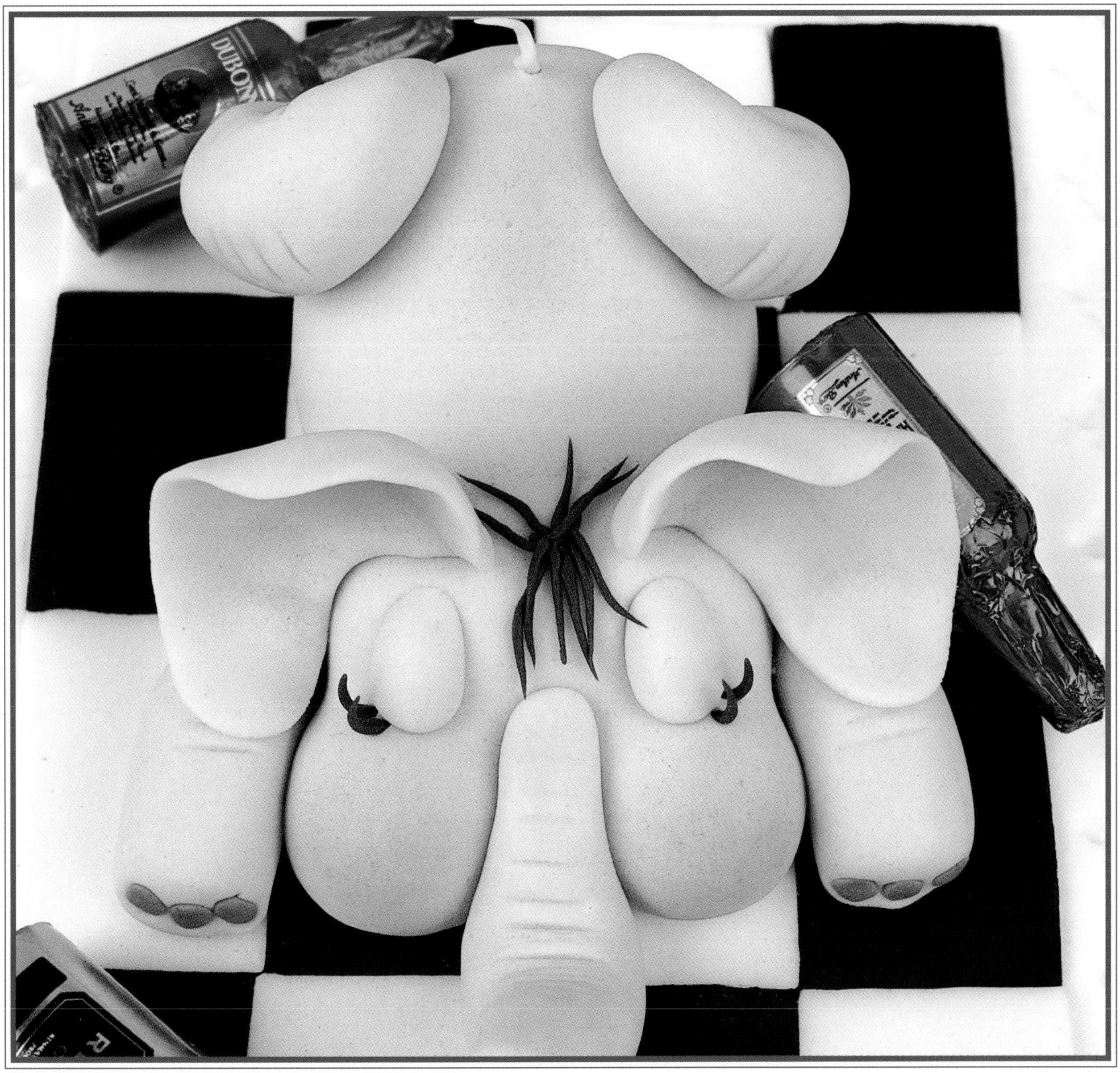

The body and head are formed from pastillage paste and then covered in a sheet of paste to finish.

ELEPHANT IN A GLASS

Gail Gambrell

erhaps the tables have been turned here. Instead of seeing pink elephants after too much sparkling wine, this little rascal got there first and now we have an elephant who has drunk too much pink bubbly.

GLASS MOULD

Use a sparkling wine glass to make the mould. Dust inside the glass with cornflour/cornstarch. Line the glass with pastillage paste and flatten down. Using a wooden toothpick or cocktail stick, push small holes around the top to prevent the mould from cracking as it dries. Leave for a short time to dry, then turn out and finish drying.

GLASS

Make a round paper pattern large enough to cover the curved surface of the glass mould. Roll out some ivory-coloured pastillage paste very thinly and use the paper pattern to cut out a circle. Place the circle over the mould and press a pattern around the edge. I used the end of a souvenir spoon to decorate my glass. Allow to dry.

GLASS STEM

Wrap seven 10 cm/4 in long strands of dry spaghetti in pastillage paste and allow to dry. You can also use a long peppermint stick to strengthen.

GLASS BASE

Press a 2.5 cm/1 in ball of pastillage paste into the bottom of a wine glass to give a 5 cm/2 in diameter circle. Turn out onto the flat side and decorate the edge to match the glass top. Brush a small amount of gum glue around one end of the dried stem. Push the stem into the centre of the base and allow to dry.

When dry attach the glass top to the stem using a small amount of royal icing and allow to dry. Brush the glass stem with gum glue.

Roll out a long sausage of pastillage paste 6 mm/¼ in thick. Neatly wrap around the stem of the glass.

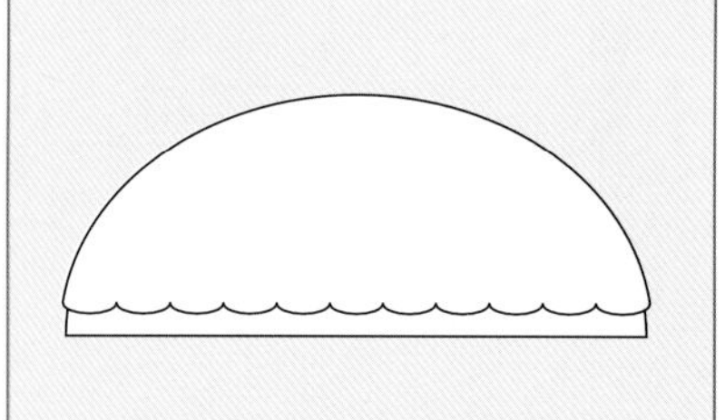

Pattern for glass top.

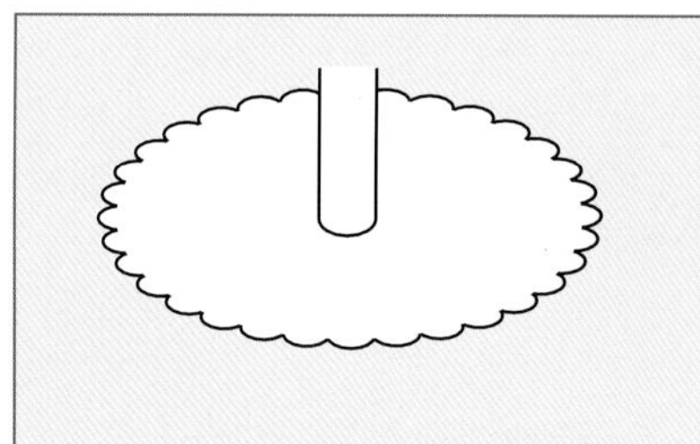

Pattern for glass base.

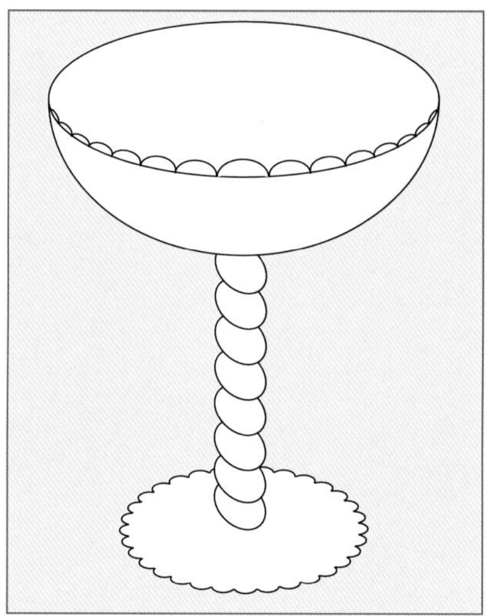

Pattern for completed glass.

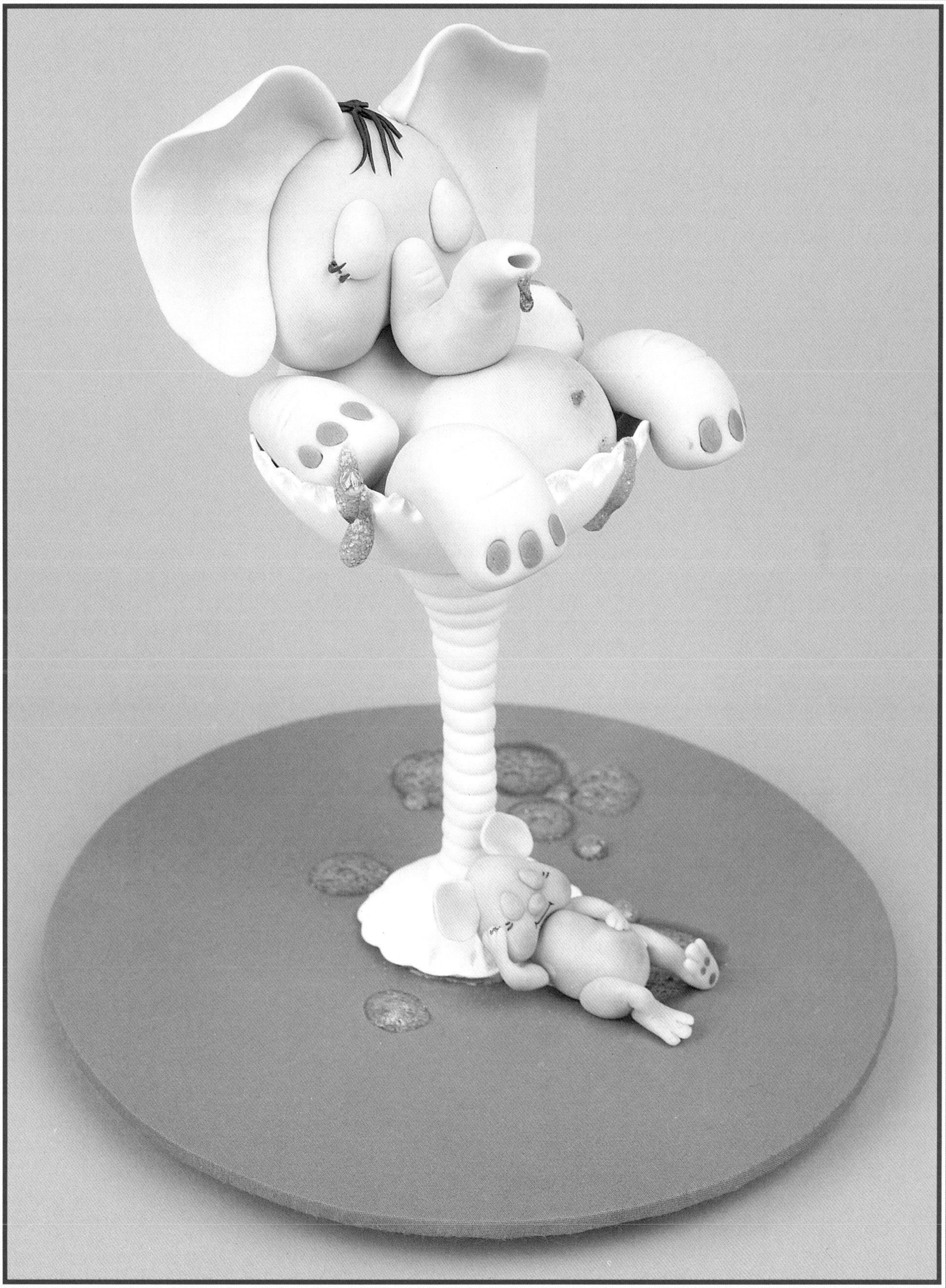

The elephant is assembled piece by piece in the glass.

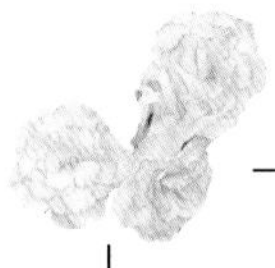

BODY

Form an oval shape using a 6.5 cm/2½ in ball of pale grey pastillage paste. Bend the oval to form a kidney shape. Place into the glass with the curved side down. Place three strands of dry spaghetti into one end of the body to hold the head.

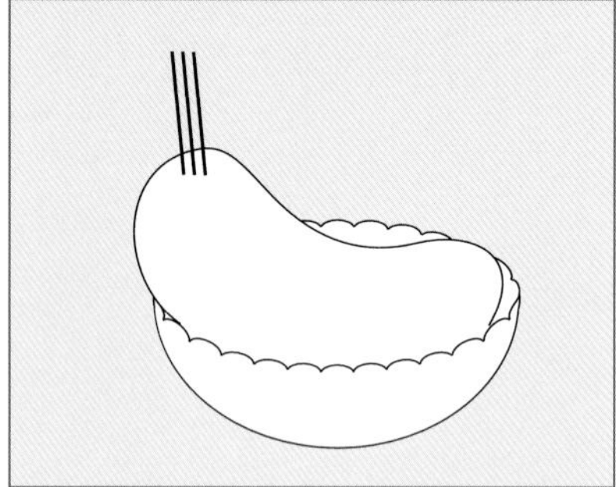

Pattern for body in glass.

HEAD

Form an egg shape using a 5 cm/2 in ball of pale grey pastillage paste. Cup in your hand and using the thumb of the cupped hand, apply slight pressure to the front base of the egg shape. This will force the two sides out to form the elephant's cheeks.

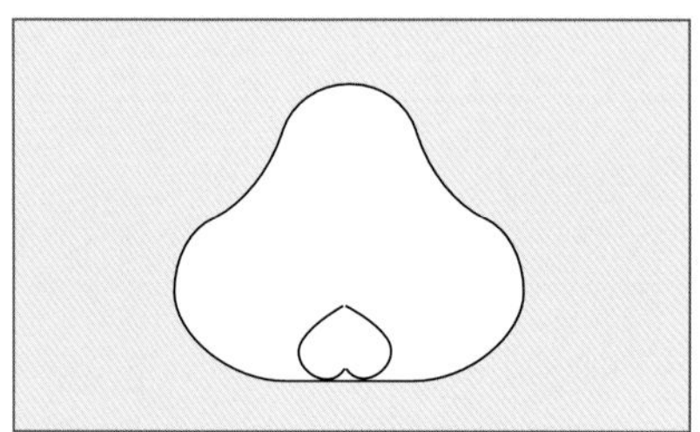

Pattern for head.

EYES

Using a medium balling tool, ball two ovals above the cheeks to form eye sockets. Using a 1.25 cm/½ in ball of pastillage paste, form an oval and place into the eye socket indent. Repeat for other eye.

Place a small amount of gum glue at the base of the elephant's head and push the head down onto the spaghetti.

Pattern for eye sockets.

TRUNK

Using a 2.5 cm/1 in ball of pastillage paste, form a 7.5 cm/3 in long sausage shape tapered at both ends. Using a small balling tool, hollow out one end of the trunk. Brush a small amount of gum glue between the elephant's cheeks and attach the other end of the trunk to the elephant's face. Rest the trunk on the chest and curve the end up. Mark creases along the trunk.

BACK LEGS

Make a cone shape using a 2.5 cm/1 in ball of pastillage paste. Using a small balling tool make three indents on the outside edge of the larger end. Fill these indents with a darker coloured grey pastillage paste to form the elephant's toe nails. Curve the leg and attach the narrow end to the side front of the elephant's body with gum glue. Hang the large end over the front of the glass.

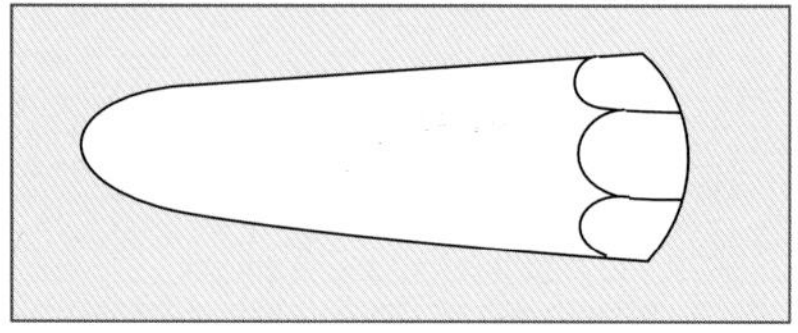

Pattern for back leg.

FRONT LEGS

Make the same way as for the back legs. Lie the legs on either side of the upper body.

EARS

Using a 2.5 cm/1 in ball of pastillage paste, form a shape similar to your own ears, wide at the top and narrow at the bottom. Attach to the elephant's head with gum glue and curve forward.

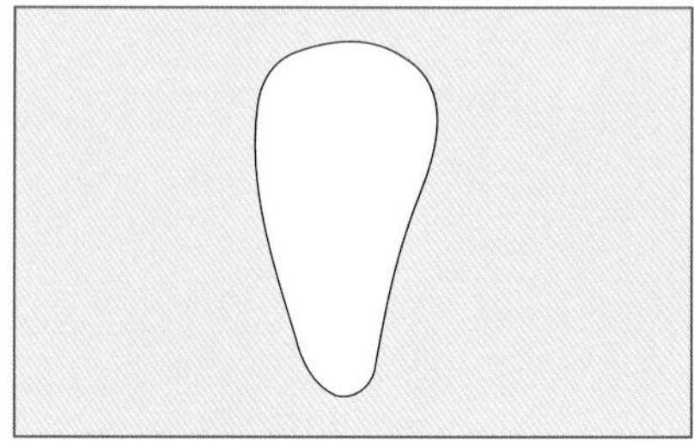

Pattern for ear.

ASSEMBLY

Make three eyelashes for each eye out of black pastillage paste and attach to the base of the elephant's eye or pipe three eyelashes with royal icing. Dust the cheeks, stomach and inside ears with pink chalk.

Make the sparkling wine by mixing together 2 teaspoons of gelatine and 2 tablespoons of water. Heat gently until the gelatine is dissolved and add 2 drops pink food colour. Beat lightly to form bubbles.

Dribble wine (gelatine) over the edge of the glass and at the base. Hang a small drip off the end of the elephant's trunk. Allow to dry.

The little fellow who has fallen asleep is made from pastillage paste, coloured and secured in position with a little royal icing.

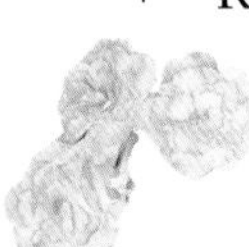

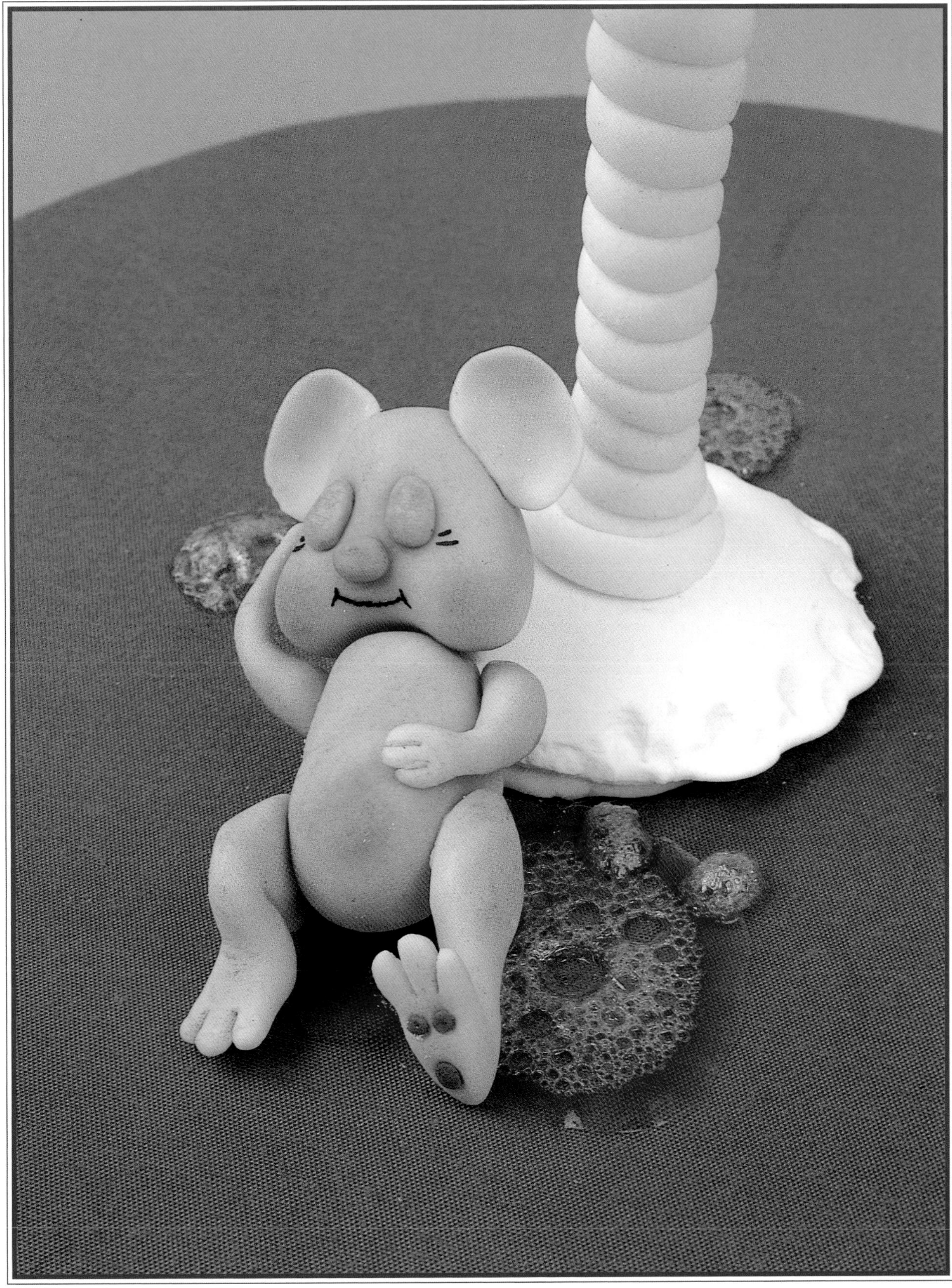

A mixture of gelatine and water is used to make the sparkling wine.

EASTER CHICKEN

Gail Gambrell

ow what better way to begin Easter Sunday than with a greeting from this chicken who has definitely outgrown his shell. Arrange your table around this captivating little face and watch the smiles. Use pastillage paste to make a 14 cm/5½ in plaque on which the chicken sits.

EGG SHELL TOP

Take a 2.5 cm/1 in ball of egg shell-coloured pastillage paste and roll out. Place the top egg shell pattern on the rolled out paste and cut out using a scalpel. Fit over the top of suitable container. I used a small egg-shaped container. Allow to dry.

Egg Shell Bottom

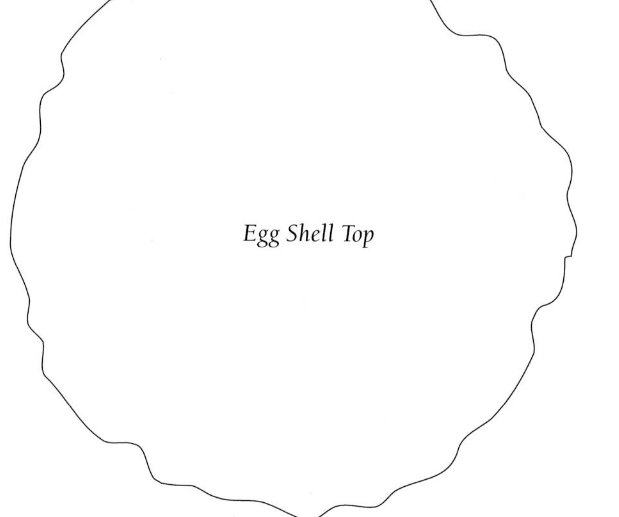

EGG SHELL BOTTOM

Repeat as for the egg top but use the bottom egg pattern. When dry attach to the centre of the plaque using a small amount of royal icing. Allow to dry. The egg shell bottom must be firmly fixed to the plaque before continuing.

Pattern for the construction of the shell and base.

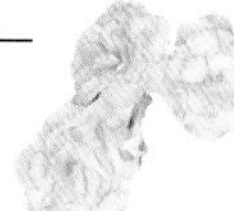

A very surprised face is the secret of this chicken's charm.

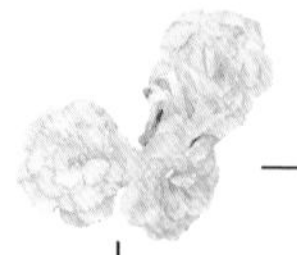

FEET

Use a 1.25 cm/½ in ball of orange pastillage paste and form two small golf stick shapes for the feet. Flatten the ends downwards and cut two wedges out of each to form the toes. Pinch the opposite sides together to form a heel. Set aside and allow to dry.

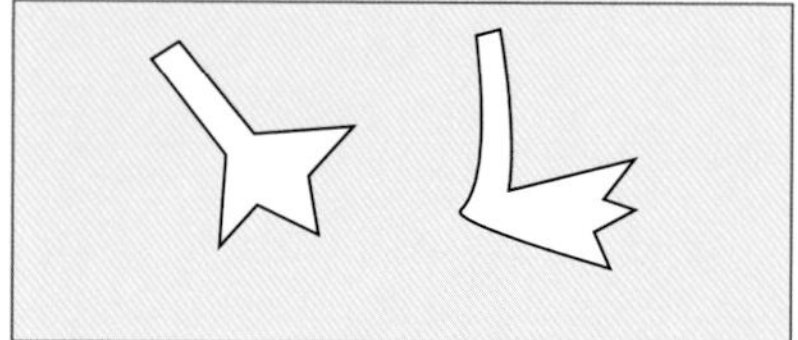

Pattern for feet.

BODY

Use approximately 5 cm/2 in ball of yellow pastillage paste and form a pear shape. Place three strands of dry spaghetti down through the top centre. Set aside on cotton wool or wadding to dry.

HEAD

Using a 2.5 cm/1 in ball of pastillage paste form a pear shape. Place the pear shape into a cupped hand with the long end of the pear shape pointing to your thumb. Press with your thumb into the fatter side of the pear shape easing out a small amount of paste either side to form the cheeks. Using a medium balling tool make two small round indents above each cheek. These form the eye sockets.

BODY ASSEMBLY

Place a small amount of royal icing into the bottom egg shell. Place the chicken's body carefully into the egg shell. Do not press too hard or the shell will break. Place the chicken's head on top of its body, pushing the spaghetti through the centre bottom of its head. The spaghetti should not show through the top of the head. The cut-out wedge of the chicken's bottom shell should be facing to the right side of the body.

WINGS

Using a 2.5 cm/1 in ball of pale yellow pastillage paste form a long pear shape then flatten. Using small sharp scissors, cut slits down one side of the wing. Attach the narrow end of the wing to the side top of the chicken's body using a small amount of moisture with the cut side of the wing facing forwards. Curve one wing up and support with wadding underneath until dry enough to stay. Curve the other wing downwards to rest on the edge of the bottom egg shell.

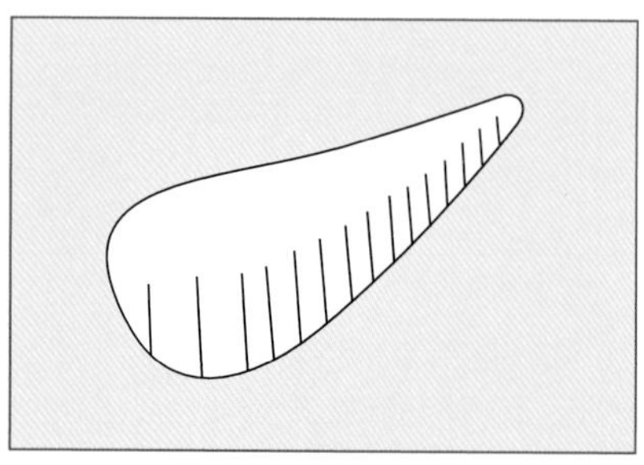

Pattern for wing.

EYES

Brush a small amount of moisture into the eye indents of the chicken's head. Using pale yellow pastillage paste form two small balls of paste and place into the eye indents. The eyes should protrude outwards from the eye sockets.

BEAK

Use a small amount of orange pastillage paste form a cone shape and flatten sideways. Using small sharp scissors cut sideways from the pointed end of the cone. Open the beak out. Place a small amount of moisture at the base of the beak and attach to the chicken's face.

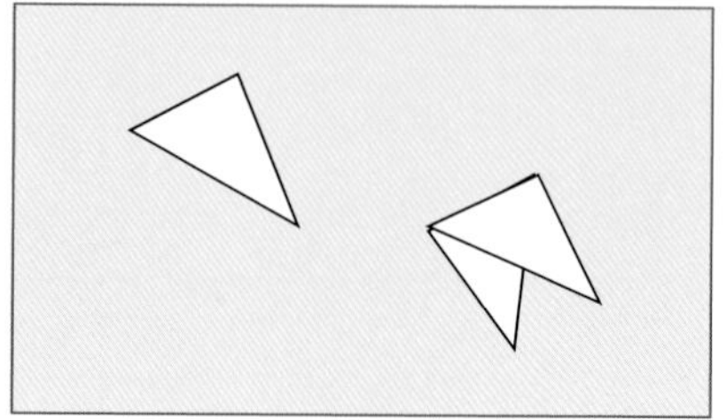

Pattern for beak.

LEGS

Form a cone shape using a 1.25 cm/½ in piece of pale yellow pastillage paste. Push one of the chicken's dried feet into the narrow end of the cone. Using a small amount of moisture attach the cone to the side of the lower body through the cut-out wedge in the bottom egg shell. Rest the chicken's foot onto the plaque. Place a small amount of royal icing onto the end of the other foot and attach to the opposite side of the bottom egg shell, resting the foot on the plaque.

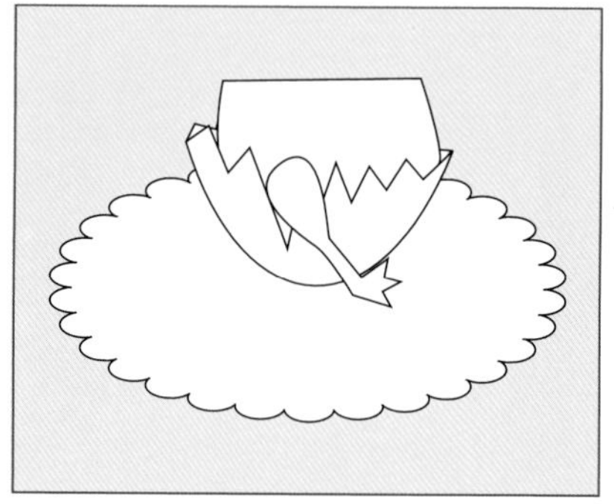

Pattern for leg position.

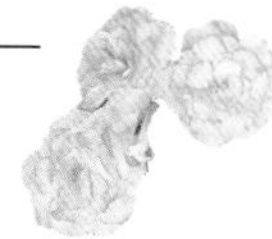

Subtle colouring and a minimum of decoration are the way to make this chicken appealing. The shell is very fragile and should be secured well with royal icing.

ASSEMBLY

Brush the chicken's cheeks with pink chalk to highlight them. Using a fine paint brush and black food colouring, paint the eye and then paint three eye lashes on the side of each eye. Place a few chocolate Easter eggs on the plaque to finish off piece.

Pattern for assembly of the Easter chicken.

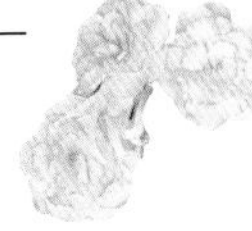

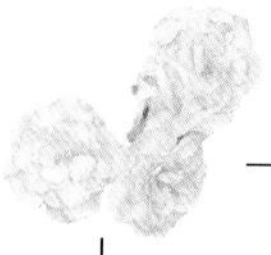

MARZIPAN FRUITS AND ANIMALS

Hervé Boutin

arzipan is mixture of almond and sugar and in Switzerland, Germany, France, the Netherlands and Belgium modelling in marzipan is an established industry with a large number of crafts people specialising in this field. In the United States, Australia and Asia it is used to a lesser degree.

The most popular shapes are fruits and figurines particularly animals. When modelling in marzipan it is necessary to work as quickly as possible before the marzipan becomes too sticky.

The basis of all good modelling begins with a suitable almond paste or marzipan.

In countries where a lot of marzipan is eaten the paste is usually higher in almond content and lower in sugar—sometimes over fifty per cent almond content. This marzipan is very soft and sticky and is difficult to mould. It also has a shorter shelf life.

The most common marzipan is made with about thirty-three per cent almond content. This is much easier to mould and stores well. Marzipan can be made with raw or cooked almond paste.

The first method consists of mixing icing/confectioner's sugar with almonds which have been previously blanched. The mixture is then ground to a paste. This marzipan is quickly made but the shelf life is limited and the flavour is considered average.

The second method, cooked marzipan, is made by preparing a syrup made from sugar, water and glucose. Cook to 120°C/250°F and mix with blanched

The bright colours are painted on or air brushed after the animals are shaped.

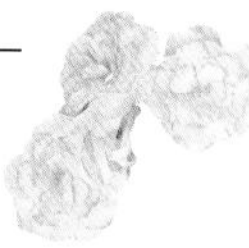

almonds. The mixture is then ground to a paste.

Marzipan can be coloured using either paste or liquid colours. Liquid colours reduce the shelf life, as humidity causes the marzipan to sweat and start a fermentation process especially with marzipan with a high level of almond content.

MARZIPAN FRUITS

You will need approximately 30 g/1 oz marzipan per fruit. Form a ball using your hands but not your fingers. From this ball you can create apples, oranges, mandarins, nectarines indeed all fruits which look like spheres.

Other fruits like pears or mangoes are shaped with a ball which is squeezed into an oval shape. Bananas are formed from a sausage shape of marzipan. The leaves are made separately and put on after colouring. The spots and other marks on the skins have been painted using a fine brush. The blush on the pears and apples is sprayed on.

ANIMALS

Each of the animals here are made from a 45 g/1½ oz marzipan ball. The eyes are added last of all after the animal is coloured. The bases of the animals have been dipped in melted chocolate.

Perfectly moulded and coloured orange and apple.

A chocolate ribbon has been added to this small piece of marzipan art.

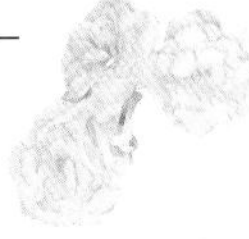

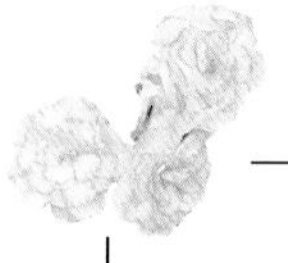

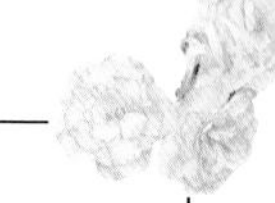

BANKSIA STUMP

Jean Cole-Clark

he banksia is an Australian native which grows profusely throughout the country with leathery leaves and large cylindrical seed pods. The dry pods are called banksia men and are immortalised in classic Australian children's literature. The pods open up in a bush fire and thus spread their seeds—nature's way of renewing the forest. They are often twisted and gnarled stumps with growth at odd angles. There are a number of different varieties.

The unusual beauty of the banksia is what led me to make this piece. Creative cake decorating is very interesting to me because so many different ideas and techniques can be used. They are generally first time ideas so there can be many disasters along the way to success. But don't let that make you put your brilliant ideas in the 'too-hard' basket. Keep at it and you will find it both challenging and rewarding.

It is a good idea to do a rough sketch of the shape and size you require for the design. This way you can see if your proportions are correct.

In creative work, boards covered with icing look good and this one was painted to look like grass, pebbles and sand appropriate to the design.

First make the cake as near as possible to the shape needed so that there are not too many joins in the final design. To make the stump you will need a large cake which can be cut into two pieces. The cake that I finally used for the stump contained twenty-five eggs. This was after experimenting with a twenty-egg flop. Cut the cake in two and rejoin for the stump using royal icing. Allow it to dry thoroughly before cutting it into the final shape with a very sharp knife.

Always cover the cake—yes I always use a cake because I like the challenge—with almond paste/marzipan first to make sure you get a good shape. It is like the undercoat when you are painting. Your top coat will only be as good as the undercoat so spend a lot of time getting it right in the first place then the rest is easy.

Mix your own colours as it is the only way to get a true match to the original. Test them before painting the cake.

Opposite and this page: This very large sculpture is made on a cake base which has been shaped and covered in marzipan before the finish was applied. *(See page 165.)*

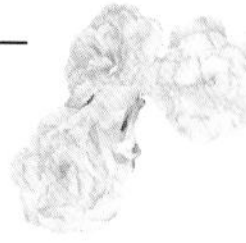

Powder colours continue to darken while drying so paint a sample and leave it for a few days. I watched the tree stump get darker by the day. Darker than I really wanted unfortunately so I decided to lighten it by brushing it with water to try and remove some of the colour. This turned out to be a good idea as it gave the weathered look which was what I really wanted. You can always learn from your mistakes.

The banksia pod, leaves, birds and nest were all made from moulding paste and coloured later. The whole piece took weeks to make but won a championship award. The main lesson I learned from all this was not to make a piece that required two men or a trolley to move around.

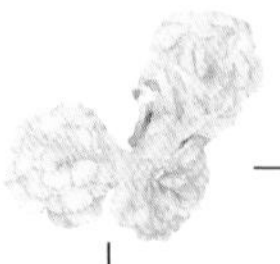

TAPESTRY BAG

Jean Cole-Clark

he idea for this unusual piece just came to me one day out of nowhere. I was tired of flora and fauna so decided to create a man-made object.

Make a 25 cm/10 in square cake and cut approximately 5 cm/2 in off one side. This should make the bag 25 cm/10 in x 20 cm/8 in. Round off the top corners with a very sharp knife. The side pocket is shaped out of the cut-off piece with the flat side against the bag. Cover the whole bag the side pocket, both sides and ends with almond paste/marzipan and smooth out.

Run a smocking roller all over the bag to give the appearance of tapestry.

Five different colours are used to paint the daisy design starting with a beige/cream background plus black, dark brown, orange, red and white. Blue is used to colour the filler flowers between the daisies.

For the straps, roll out strips of moulding paste 2.5 cm/1 in wide and mark lengthwise with the smocking roller. Make end loops and attach rings made from moulding paste.

To make the zippers, press a real zipper into a strip of moulding paste. Attach at the top and side. Make a zipper tab out of moulding paste.

Roll out the piping for the bag from moulding paste and attach to the bag on the joins and where shown on the pattern. Roll out a long strip for the strap and mark lengthwise with a smocking roller. Attach through the end piece, through the buckle, around the other end and back to the buckle.

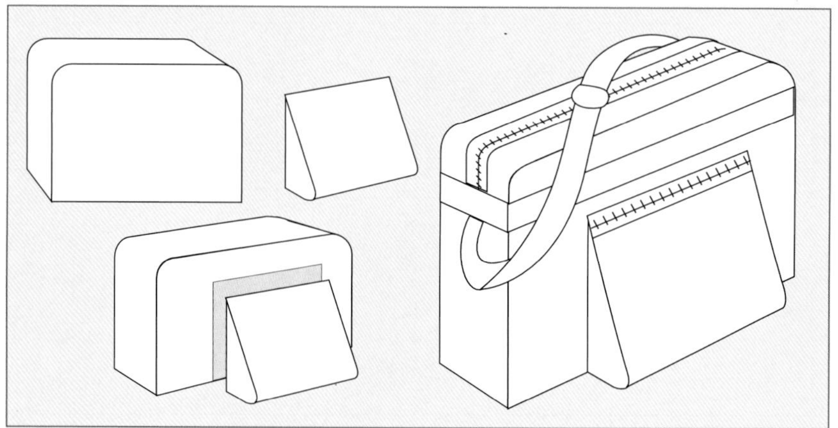

Design for construction of the bag.

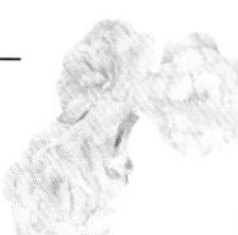

Superb painting of the daisies is the feature of this colourful bag.

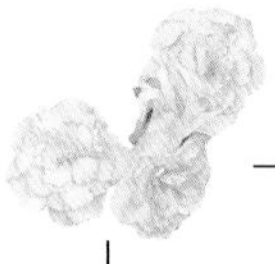

DRAPES

Lynette Speer

rapes are now being used often in cake decorating and expertly made they can look as soft as any fabric.

Cover the cake and board as desired. Plan design, make the necessary templates and transfer the markings onto the cake. Finish the lower edge of the cake with a piped beading, pipe any embroidery and attach ribbon.

Use fondant, with a little moulding paste added if necessary, and roll out thinly and straighten the edges.

Use cocktail sticks, wooden toothpicks, skewers or knitting needles depending on the size of the drape you require. Slide the first stick under the sheet of fondant. Place the second stick on top of the sheet but next to the first stick. Pull the sticks close together along the full length of the fondant. Continue in this way until the required number of folds are formed. Hold the ends of the sticks and turn over the drape. Trim the long sides, dampen the edges and turn in to neaten. Turn the drape right side up and carefully remove the sticks.

Place the drape over the template and gently ease to shape. Crimp the ends together with your fingers and trim to the required size.

Turn over and dampen the wrong side with water or glue. Attach to the side of the cake. Adjust where necessary to cover any placement marks.

Add icing, ribbon bows or small flowers to conceal any joins in the drapes.

VARIATIONS

Use the same size sticks for a gathered effect or use thin sticks on top and thick sticks underneath for a full drape.

Make longer drapes and crimp folds together in two or three places between joins.

Attach a garret frill to the side of the cake then position the drape over the frill.

Attach lace pieces to the lower edge of the drape.

Small symmetrical drapes finish the lower edge of this cake. *(See page 183.)*

Variations on traditional drapes.

A long elegant drape finished with a large bow is the highlight of this cake. *(See page 177.)*

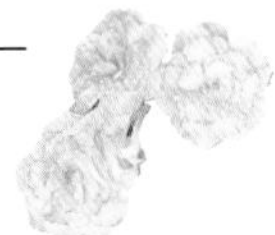

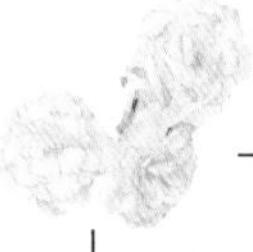

PAINTING WITH ROYAL ICING

Lorraine Wells

he art of painting with royal icing has developed from years of doing floodwork and adapting a few basic art techniques. The consistency of the royal icing used for painting depends on the effect you are after.

The best consistency is similar to thin honey for painting skies, water and buildings. Shading and outlining is also done using a soft brush and a very thin honey consistency. A no. 00 or 0 brush lightly dipped in the royal icing is ideal when outlining your work. The use of soft and flat brushes helps to give different textures to your picture.

Prepare the cake or plaque and allow to dry. Draw or trace the illustration and reduce or enlarge to fit the cake. Transfer the design onto the cake. As for floodwork, the background is the first to be painted.

THE SKY

Add enough water to royal icing to make it the consistency of thin honey. Mix several shades of pale blue on the palette. Apply the coloured icing, blending the shades of blue as you paint.

For clouds, use the palest blue/mauve or white, thin royal icing. Paint in the clouds while the sky is still wet.

THE DISTANT HILLS

Use the same consistency as for the sky. The most distant hill is painted in a pale blue/mauve colour. The next hill may be a green/grey tone.

THE TREES BEHIND THE HOUSE

The tree trunks are painted first in a grey/brown colour and when dry the tree tops are painted using several shades of green. Use a stiff flat brush about 6 mm/$\frac{1}{4}$ in wide. Lightly dip the tip into the royal icing and apply to the tree top area, holding the brush at 90° angle to work. Use a dabbing action to give a leaf effect.

THE HOUSE

Use the thin consistency royal icing. Paint the front wall first. When dry paint the side wall, windows and doors. Paint the roof and chimney and under the eaves. Allow to dry before painting in the lines on the roof and eaves.

The verandah posts, door and window surrounds are all painted using the very thin consistency royal icing.

HILLS AND SLOPES

Use the thin consistency royal icing and paint in the desired shades and colours.

Opposite: A very authentic country scene is hand painted in royal icing.

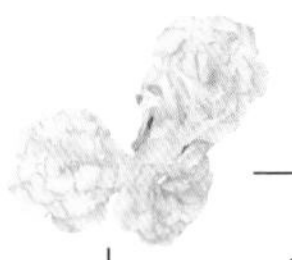

THE BUSHES IN FRONT OF THE HOUSE

Use the same method as for the tree tops behind the house and paint in shades of green.

THE TREE TRUNKS

Paint these in a grey/brown royal icing. The knots in the trunk are painted using a deeper shade and a fine brush.

THE WATER AREA

Paint using the thin royal icing. As you paint the blue water, work in a little white royal icing to give lighter areas.

THE FENCE POSTS

Mix the colour for the fence posts into very thin royal icing. Use a no. 00 or 0 sable brush to paint the fence posts and wire. Be careful not to put too much icing on the brush.

THE ROCKS AND SHADING

Use a dark brown gradually blending to a lighter shade to give texture.

Allow the picture to dry completely then mix the colours needed for outlining and shading. Paint in the reeds around the water edge and grass tufts where needed, e.g. at the base of the tree trunks and fence posts.

To shade, you need the same consistency of royal icing as for outlining. Use a soft brush and apply shading. If you wish to go over the shading be sure to allow each layer to dry thoroughly between each coat. After completing the shading, use a no. 0 sable brush to outline the picture.

THE GRASS

To paint short grass, work with a stiff brush lightly dipped in thin royal icing. Work the brush strokes from the base upwards. This will give the effect of grass blades.

All these methods can be practised on art paper before beginning on the cake. Royal icing painting forms a thinner layer than floodwork and will not soak into art paper.

The sides of this cake have a continuous mural running around them.

The stippled effect on the trees gives a realistic look to the scene on this cake.
The background is completed before beginning on the trees.

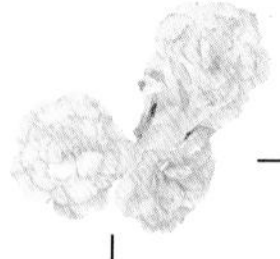

BOY AND GIRL PLAQUE

Julia Kook

perfect keepsake that will last for years, this plaque can be made in any design. After completion it can be framed to suit the room or placed on a cake.

Make a plaque from a mixture of half moulding paste and half plastic icing. Ensure that the surface is completely dry before proceeding. Sketch or trace the basic outline of the picture onto the plaque.

Cut out a stencil for the background in acetate and place over the plaque. Use chalk or an airbrush to apply the background colour to the plaque. Finer details are then painted in using a fine paint brush and paste food colours. The second layer of the background is flooded with royal icing to give a slightly higher dimension to the design.

The flowers in the tub are stippled to give a textured effect. Finish the background by adding flowers cut from moulding paste. The picture frames are also cut from moulding paste.

The boy and girl are made next. The faces are made using a plastic mould with moulding paste. Set aside to dry. Use a fine brush to paint in the faces.

Form the body shapes from moulding paste and clothe while still soft. This helps keep the soft contours in the bodies. The hair can be cut from moulding paste or piped using royal icing.

The plaque is finished with an edge of fine lace. It can be displayed on a velvet-covered board and finished off with a picture frame, either wooden or made from icing.

A spray of roses and leaves made from moulding paste completes the picture. The roses are made using various sizes of all-in-one five-petal blossom cutters. Loops of satin ribbon complete the picture.

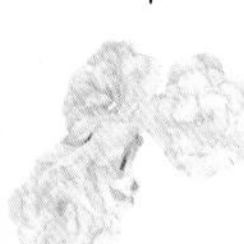

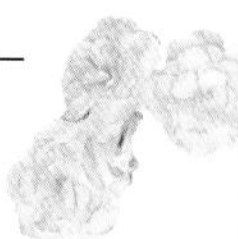

A perfect gift, this plaque is made using the bas-relief method and can be used as a cake top or a wall plaque.

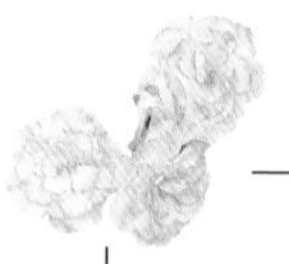

MOUSE PLAQUE

Julia Kook

his extremely cute plaque is a favourite with all children and brings a charming country cottage feel to a room. The theme of the plaque can be designed around a favourite book or cartoon character or toy.

The plaque is made from a mixture of half moulding paste and half plastic icing. The surface must be completely dry before anything is added. Trace the outline of the design onto the surface of the plaque.

Begin with the background which is coloured with chalk. An airbrush can be used if you prefer. Cut out a stencil in acetate to shield any parts of the background you do not wish coloured.

The drawers, mirror and picture frames are flooded onto the surface after the background is thoroughly dry. Add a picture frame made from moulding paste.

The mother mouse, baby and owl are moulded separately. Place the baby and owl on the plaque when dry. The blanket, crib cover and curtain have been cut from moulding paste and added to the plaque. Add the mother mouse last of all.

When the main items are in place use a fine brush to paint in the detail. Pipe on a long tail and apron strings. The flowers are made from moulding paste using blossom cutters. The whole piece has been mounted on a velvet background and then framed in a natural timber.

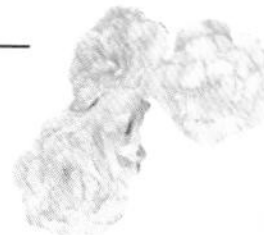

This plaque is made by building up layers of moulding paste shapes. The method is called bas-relief.

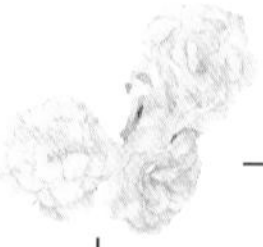

FLORAL PILLAR

Barbara Batterham

his method of creating three-dimensional work on pillars allows the beautiful clear acrylic or glass pillars to be seen to advantage and adds another dimension to floral work on cakes.

Cover the base of the pillar with finely rolled moulding paste coloured to match the fondant on the cake. Roll out the paste thinly, moisten the bottom of the pillar and place it on the rolled paste. Trim around neatly with a scalpel then turn it over to check for any air bubbles. It may be necessary to trim the edges once again so the paste will not be noticed when in position on the cake. Allow to dry and harden and then the edges can be smoothed with a file.

WILD ROSE—FLOWER 1

Cut five wild rose petals from very thinly rolled moulding paste. Shape, flute and cup each petal. Colour with chalk or alcohol colouring. Roll a very thin sausage for a stem, moisten one side and shape high up on the pillar, firming in position. Alternately the stems may be piped. Lie the pillar on its side on a piece of foam, and begin laying the five petals on the stem to form a rose on the inside of the pillar. Moisten the back of each petal in turn, and the front of the petal it will overlap. Tuck the last petal under the first and firm. Place in position inside the pillar. Cotton wool may be needed to support petals. Leave to dry overnight.

Make a centre for the rose from fine cotton and fix a tiny green ball in the middle. Lightly touch the ends with egg white and dip in cornmeal/polenta. When the rose is dry, attach the centre with a small amount of royal icing or egg white. Colouring can be used once the paste is dry, using care to keep the pillar very clean. A small damp paint brush or a brush dipped in alcohol can be used to clean off any marks that appear.

To complete this rose, cut a calyx from green paste, thin and ball each sepal and moisten in the centre only. Attach this calyx on the outside of the pillar, positioning it over the centre of the inside rose. Make a small hip and attach it to the centre of the calyx.

This can also be reversed with the petals on the outside and the calyx on the inside of the pillar.

LEAVES

Leaves are rolled and cut from moulding paste, veined, shaped and coloured and added to the stem in a natural way. Leaves should also be attached to the inside of the pillar, back to back with those on the outside. Buds can be added also.

Flowers can hang down as well, showing the backs of the petals only together with a calyx and rosehip. This rose

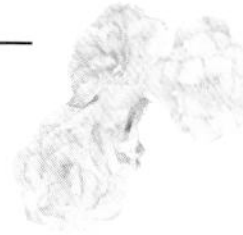

would have three petals on the outside of the pillar with the calyx, hip and stem. The remaining rose petal would be placed on the inside of the pillar, competing the flower. Other flower sprays can be built up in the same way.

HANGING ROSE—FLOWER 2

This rose is made in a similar way to the first but it has half the petals on the inside and the other half on the outside of the pillar. Begin the rose by making the rosehip. Make a small green rosehip from moulding paste. Leave to dry. Cut out a small green calyx, trim and leave only three sepals. Ball and shape each sepal, moisten the centre and position on the dried rosehip with the sepals lying backwards. Allow this to dry before continuing.

Cut three petals—two the same size as before and another slightly larger. Ball and shape each petal. Moisten the base of the larger petal and position it on the centre of the calyx allowing it to rest back over the calyx. Take both the smaller petals and attach them, with their points all meeting in the centre, in the same way. Gently fold over the top side of these petals and with a soft brush coax the larger petal over the others. The effect should show a small soft indentation in the larger petal where it joins the calyx, making it appear real. When dry attach a small centre of cotton using royal icing.

The other half of the rose is made in the same way, beginning with the hip. Cut two points off a calyx, ball and attach to the hip with the points up. Leave to dry before attaching two or three shaped petals as before. A small centre of stamens is positioned before folding the petals down. The rose should appear as a complete flower when looking through the pillar walls from any angle.

Small filler flowers and rosebuds are made in the same manner. Stems can be piped, cut or rolled—my preference is piped because they are so much finer and thorns can be added. Stems form the framework of the picture and bring all the flowers together.

Leaves should be made as for the first rose and attached both inside and outside the pillar. Allow to dry before colouring.

Many flowers can be created in this way. If you have the patience, tiny flowers such as violets, with each petal made separately, are a delight. This idea needn't be restricted to flowers—virtually any idea you have can become a reality.

ATTACHING THE PILLAR

The skewers used to secure the pillar can be painted on the top, and I have found white correction fluid easy to use for this. The pillar is positioned on the cake and secured with royal icing. The skewers should not be visible.

The roses and buds on this pillar are formed inside and outside the pillar walls. (See page 191.)

SECTION FOUR

ROYAL PIPING

TULLE WORK

FILIGREE

UNSUPPORTED PIPEWORK

Swans • Butterfly • Tower • Church

ENTWINED SWANS

Adèle Humphrys

hese delicate entwined swans make a lasting memento for a special occasion. They can be displayed alone or placed on a special cake or centrepiece. They are made from stiffened cotton tulle which is covered all over with cornelli work.

The first step is to draw or trace a pattern for the swans. From this make a pattern of the tulle pieces required. The tulle pieces for these swans are joined so that they form a single decoration.

Take your time and leave plenty of overlap when you first start. It can always be trimmed off later but it gives greater freedom to form the swans gracefully.

When you are happy with the design, stiffen the cotton tulle pieces and join with small amounts of royal icing. Using a very fine piping tube, pipe all over the swans in fine cornelli work. Don't cover all the tulle, the idea is to see through the decoration but make sure that your pipework covers any joins in the tulle.

The beaks are shaped in royal icing and attached to the swans. The eyes are piped on last of all. Allow to dry thoroughly.

Prepare the board and pipe on a little royal icing to hold the swans. Carefully place the swans in position. Add any flowers or other adornment you wish.

These exquisite swans are formed from stiffened tulle covered with fine cornelli work.

TULLE CHURCH

Adèle Humphrys

s a decoration on its own or as part of a cake top, this tulle church provides an interesting focal point. By altering the colour and texture of the windows and the cornelli work this church can be made to blend with the colour scheme of almost any wedding.

First draw or trace a design for the church. Next make a pattern from this and cut out each piece in cotton tulle, i.e. sides, roof, gables and spire. Stiffen each piece, place over desired shape or curve and allow to dry. Form the cone for the spire and leave to dry.

Using a very fine piping tube, decorate each piece with fine cornelli work. Leave to dry. Cut out window panes from desired colour and attach to the inside of the windows with a little royal icing. Pipe a finishing edge around the outside of the windows.

Make a base for the church from moulding paste. Begin assembly of the church by joining the gables to the roof and then the roof to the sides. Allow each section to dry before proceeding. Place on the base and pipe a finishing edge around the edge. Place the spire in position and attach with a little royal icing.

Pipe a lace edge around the whole roof. Other piping may be used to finish off the raw edges if you prefer. Finally pipe the cross for the spire and when thoroughly dry attach to the top of the spire with a little royal icing.

Above: The windows in the church are positioned before joining the sides. Opposite: A real fairytale atmosphere is created by the adornment of a tulle-based cornelli work church. *(See page 179.)*

FLYING BIRDS

Adèle Humphrys

The extremely low weight of these tulle birds enables them to be easily suspended above or balanced within an arrangement. The position of the wings is easily altered to suit, as these are attached separately.

Make a pattern for the birds and then cut out the tulle pieces. Stiffen the tulle and then join up the pieces to make the birds' bodies. The wings are made separately.

Use a very fine piping tube to decorate the birds and wings with fine cornelli work. Pipe a beak and eyes on each bird.

Attach the wings using a little royal icing. The birds on this cake are suspended on the long stems protruding from the orchids. They are carrying a lucky horseshoe made from royal icing and linked with a strand of lemon satin ribbon.

The construction of the birds on tulle makes them so light that they almost fly away with the lucky horseshoe. *(See page 189.)*

HORSE AND CARRIAGE

Adèle Humphrys

areful construction of the horse and carriage on tulle with the wheels being flooded is the secret of this magical fairytale piece.

Draw or trace the pattern for the whole piece. Next cut out the individual elements of the design and cut these pieces out of cotton tulle. Stiffen all the tulle pieces. Assemble the individual parts of the pattern, joining the tulle with royal icing. Take care when shaping each piece and check your original design as you go.

Draw a pattern for the wheels. Cover the pattern with non-stick transparent paper or baking paper and using a fine piping tube, pipe the outline of the wheels.

Using the piping tube, push the icing into the wheel shape keeping the tube under the surface until the required look is achieved. Carefully remove the tube without leaving a trail. Finish off with a slightly damp brush. Allow to dry.

Use royal icing to assemble the horse and carriage and pipe fine cornelli work over the whole piece taking care to cover any joins. Allow to dry then carefully position on the cake board. Pipe on the reins last of all.

The perfect way to transport the bride, this horse and carriage are made from tulle with flooded wheels. *(See page 189.)*

FLAMINGOES

Adèle Humphrys

hese elegant birds are magnificent alone as a centrepiece or as an addition to a cake. They can be scaled up or down in size to suit individual requirements.

Make a pattern for the birds. Cut out the individual pieces of tulle and stiffen. Form the bodies and join with a little royal icing. Using a fine piping tube, cover the tulle bodies in fine cornelli work.

The legs are made separately from moulding paste. Allow them to dry thoroughly before attaching to the completed tulle bodies.

To create a better overall balance the beaks are painted and shaped with soft royal icing. The bodies are slightly elongated at the base to allow for a secure join to the legs. The beaks and legs are coloured in the palest pink.

The bodies of the flamingoes are made from stiffened tulle on moulding paste legs.

CRANES

Adèle Humphrys

hape and form are the things that give these birds their elegance. Care taken to prepare a good pattern will ensure that the tulle bodies are light and strong.

From the prepared pattern, cut out the tulle. Leave plenty of overlap and trim later if required. Stiffen and form into the shape you desire. It is fiddly work but worth the effort. When completed these cranes seem to float.

Join the tulle with royal icing making sure that the joins are strong otherwise the birds will not stand up.

Use a fine piping tube to pipe cornelli work all over the bodies taking care to cover the joins. Allow to dry thoroughly then arrange on a plaque or precovered cake.

The cranes can be coloured to match any other existing decoration on the cake.

An excellent feel for shape is the secret of these cranes.

FILIGREE

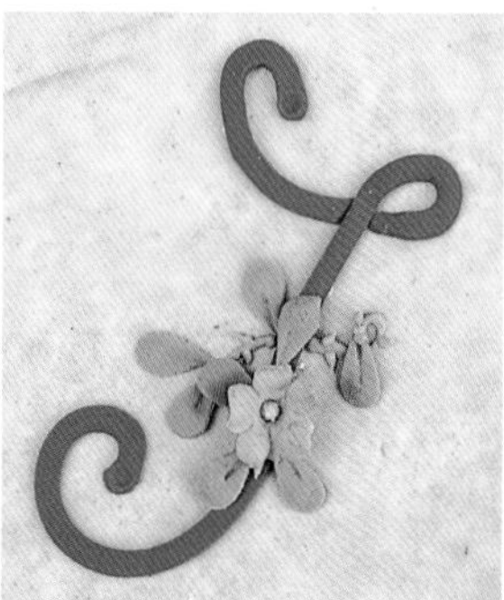

iligree work is exquisite and much easier to make than it looks. However, when beginning, work on small designs like butterflies and work up to side pieces and curves. When attaching filigree to a cake make sure that the covering is straight-sided so that the filigree pieces will fit exactly.

First draw or trace the pattern. Securely fix the pattern to a firm surface. It can be flat, curved or angled, depending on the finished result you desire. Cover the design with non-stick transparent paper or baking paper and stick it down firmly—it wrinkles when you pipe on it.

Filigree is basically lace on a larger scale and it is piped in the same way as lace with each line touching the next to give strength. The piping can be done in different weights. Filigree looks great with a heavier weight edge and fine lattice work in the centre.

Practise with a no. 0 piping tube and progress to a no. 00 piping tube for extra fineness. Remember, too open a design is not strong so fill in the spaces with curves and curls. All pieces of filigree should be identical.

When forming fine pipework, don't put too much icing in the bag. Your hand will soon tire trying to squeeze a large amount. Use only a small amount and twist the bag to give extra push and don't hold the pipe like a pen. Experiment until your hand is comfortable.

Leave a day or two to dry then remove from the surface and peel the paper off the filigree. Lay carefully on foam or wadding until ready to use. For extra strength pipe over the inside of the outside edge. Attach to the cake using a tiny amount of royal icing.

Above: This form of filigree is shaped over a curved surface. It is left to dry and then attached to the cake with a little royal icing. (Adele Humphrys.)

Right: The filigree wings are the perfect adornment to any cake. (Mavis Mepham.)

BUTTERFLY

Mavis Mepham

simple butterfly exquisitely piped is all that is needed on some cakes. When it is the only adornment, the work must be without fault and this cutie is a perfect example. A butterfly can also be used to enhance a floral decoration or to give a feeling of lightness and gentility.

Draw a design for the butterfly. Reduce or enlarge the pattern to fit the area on the cake that you wish to fill. Proportion is important because the butterfly must look like it belongs in amongst the flowers or other decoration that is on the cake.

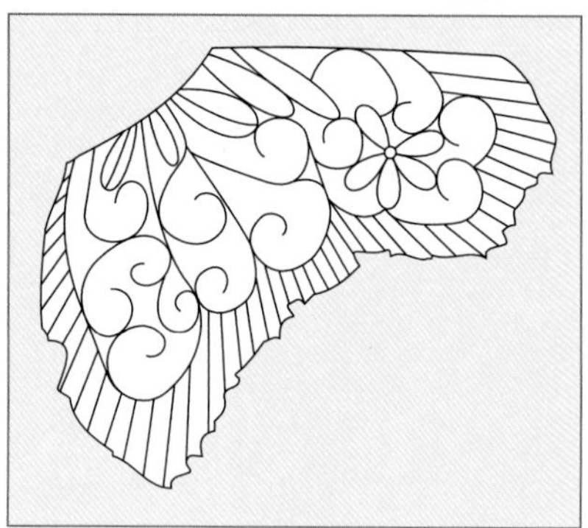

Detail of piping in the butterfly's wings.

Draw the detail of the wing pattern and reverse for the other side. Lay the pattern on a firm surface and cover with non-stick transparent paper. Secure firmly.

Using a thick no. 1 piping tube and royal icing, pipe the body of the butterfly. Mark the length of the body with creases and then mark up the face. Push two stamens in place for antennae and allow to dry.

Using a fine piping tube and royal icing, pipe the outline of one wing. Then using a finer piping tube, pipe the inside design of the wing making sure that all the piping is linked.

Repeat this for the reverse wing and allow them both to dry for twenty-four hours.

To construct the butterfly, pipe a little royal icing on the inside edge of the wing and attach to the body. Support with cotton wool or foam and allow to dry. Repeat this for the other side.

When the whole thing is thoroughly dry, mark the position of the butterfly on the cake. Pipe a little royal icing along the base of the body and gently place in position. A butterfly like this is one of the items that all sugar artists should master.

The only decoration on this cake is a perfect filigree butterfly with a piped body.

CHURCH

Kath Swansbra

he pinnacle of this prize winning cake is the tiny church at its peak. Reached by a miniature ladder it is made with unsupported pipework. It has a stained glass window and contains matching wedding rings.

Draw up the design for the church and scale to fit the size of the cake. It should be small and in proportion to the rest of the decorations. Leave a space for the windows on each side.

The church is made in pieces and then joined up. The walls are filigree and the roof and spire are brush floodwork.

Secure the pattern pieces for the walls to a firm surface and cover with non-stick transparent paper or baking paper. Using a small bag and a fine piping tube, pipe the outline of the first pattern piece. Pipe the inside links to resemble a lattice pattern. Complete each piece in a similar fashion. Allow to dry overnight.

Secure the pattern pieces for the roof and spire. Pipe the outline and complete the pieces in brush floodwork. When very dry—this can take several days—join together with royal icing. Again allow to dry thoroughly as these pieces are very very fragile.

Cut out the transparent pieces that will form the panes of glass. These can be made from gelatine or very thin rice paper or be purchased sheets in whatever colour you wish. The stained glass pattern is hand-painted onto the sheet before it is attached to the window space with a little royal icing. Allow to dry.

Pipe a little royal icing down one edge of the first wall and then place the adjoining wall in position. Support until dry. Continue in this way, gradually constructing the four walls. Join the four pieces of the spire and allow to dry. Join the two roof pieces and allow to dry.

Pipe a little royal icing around the upper edges. Place the rings in position then fit the roof and allow to dry. When thoroughly dry and strong, attach the spire with a little royal icing. Delicate lace or other finish can be piped around the whole edge if you wish. Attach the dried church to the cake with royal icing.

Opposite: This filigree and flooded church has a stained glass window and matching wedding rings inside. *(See page 169.)*

THE TOWER

Eileen Scriven

his masterpiece is made without support. It stands alone by joining each side with royal icing. Because it is made entirely of icing and ribbon it is necessary to allow each step to dry thoroughly before proceeding. The pipework must be perfect or your tower will be structurally unsound. It can be used as an addition to other creations or as a single dramatic showpiece. The pipework is completed in three stages.

Make a pattern for the tower using the illustrations. You will need a base for each level and a pattern for each side of the three levels.

Pattern for top level of the piped tower.

STAGE 1

Attach these pattern pieces to a large flat surface. Cover the pattern pieces with non-stick transparent paper or baking paper ready for overpiping. Place 1 mm/$^1/_{16}$ in ribbon in position on the pattern pieces and secure firmly. Using a no. 0 or 1 piping tube and royal icing, pipe all four pieces for each level of the tower following all lines neatly and evenly. Leave aside to dry for about twenty-four hours

You will need to add a bolt to each cross bar. Ninety-six bolts are required. For each bolt, take a very small ball of moulding paste and flatten slightly using a small pin head. Leave to dry.

You will need ninety-six bolts to complete the tower.

For the bases roll out moulding paste very thinly and cut one of each. Leave aside to dry for twenty-four hours.

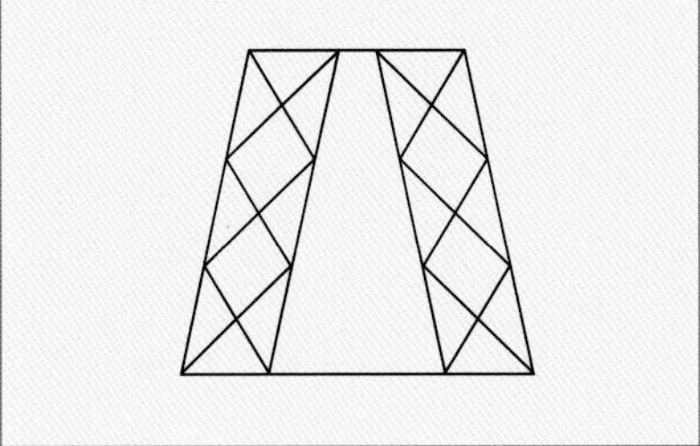

Pattern for middle level of the tower.

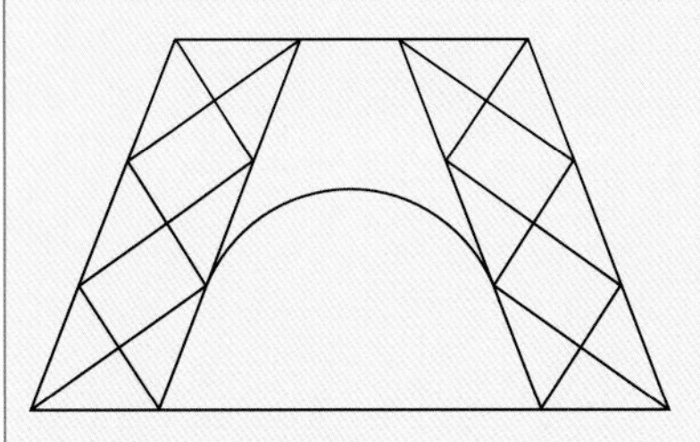

Pattern for base level of the tower.

STAGE 2

Attach the bolts in position on all cross bars as illustrated. Carefully remove the dried side pieces from the paper. Use runny royal icing to anchor the four side pieces for each level in position on the appropriate base. Leave each section to dry for a further twenty-four hours.

STAGE 3

To assemble, place all the dry sections into position and join with a little royal icing or edible glue. Extra detail can be used to conceal the joins and finish the top.

This magnificent example of pipework is unsupported by wire and is made with royal icing and ribbon.

SECTION FIVE

FLOWER MOULDING IN SUGAR PASTE

LEAVES

FLOWERS

BUDS

Australian Natives • Orchids • Seed Pods

GUMNUTS

Linda McGlinn

hese gumnuts are the ripe seed pods from eucalyptus trees. They offer a great change from the distinctly feminine designs usually seen. They are easily made, contain no wire and look fabulous alone or combined with a flooded picture.

Roll a small piece of moulding paste into a ball and place it on the pointed end of a wooden skewer. The size of the ball will determine the size of the finished gumnut.

Using your fingers pull the bottom edge of the paste down the skewer. Trim the edge if necessary. Pull up a little tail on the top of the ball of paste. Remove the gumnut from the skewer and allow dry.

If the surface of the gumnut cracks while drying don't worry because the colour will fill these cracks and give the nut an aged and weathered appearance which is quite common in the wild.

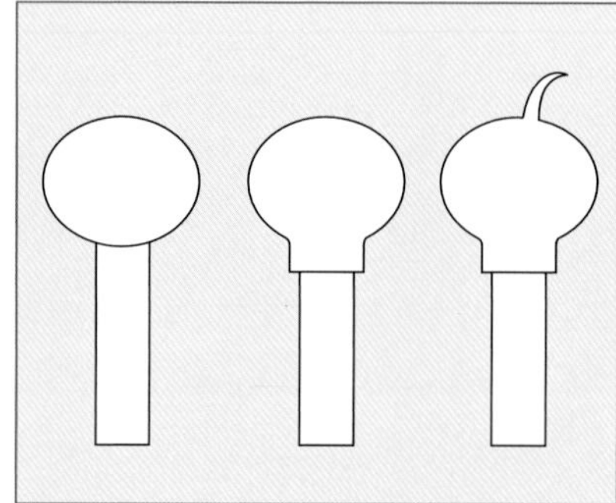

Positioning of the moulding paste on a wooden skewer.

Paint the nuts with liquid food colour. The Australian bush is full of gumnuts in a huge variety of colours from soft greens and creams to dark browns so don't worry too much about colour variations.

The leaves are cut from moulding paste. All gum leaves are strong and a little leathery. They are dusky pink when very young, then turn to soft greens and finally brown when they are ready to fall off the tree. Eucalyptus, or gum trees as they are commonly called, are evergreens and lose their leaves randomly throughout the year.

Gumnuts are hard wooden-like short cones that ripen from a green bud.

Australian natives are an excellent choice for striking plaques.

MOUNTAIN DEVIL

Eileen Scriven

his beautiful shrub, honey flower—*Lambertia formosa*, is found in the heaths and dry forest areas of New South Wales an eastern state of Australia. It flowers most of the year and has an unusual seed pod which is commonly called a mountain devil.

FLOWER BRACTS

Hook a length of medium gauge wire, moisten and cover with moulding paste. Roll to a sausage shape approximately 2.5 cm/1 in long and 2 mm/$^1/_8$ in diameter. Groove the sides and insert a length of deep pink stamen into the top end. This will be the centrepiece. Allow to dry overnight. Make six similar moulding paste sausages with grooves but without wire or stamens. Allow to dry overnight.

Moisten the dry centrepiece and place the six additional pieces in position around it taking care to keep them even. Allow to dry and then colour all seven pieces in deep red.

Add a tiny circle of white moulding paste to the top of each rolled piece. Do this by rolling moulding paste around a wooden toothpick or cocktail stick. Cut tiny thin rings which become the circles.

The bracts of flowers are grouped in threes—each group containing one long flower of about 5 cm/2 in then five more graduating from 2.5–1.25 cm/ 1-$^1/_2$ in. Curve each long length and attach in position with two close together around the base of the centre. Add other bracts directly over the long bracts as illustrated. You should have five thicknesses in groups of three. Colour the bases in red shading out to lemon/lime tips.

BUD

Hook a length of medium gauge wire and insert into moulding paste 2.5 cm /1 in long shaped like a cigar. Cut grooves and a calyx along the sides. Colour dark green at the base shading out to pale green at the tip.

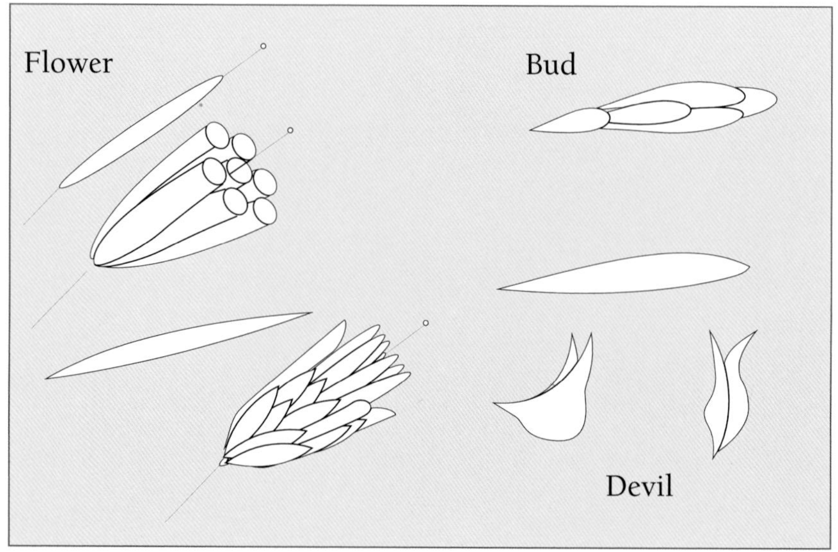

Patterns and positioning of the different parts of the mountain devil.

LEAVES

Take a length of medium gauge wire and insert into a 2.5 cm/ 1 in sausage of moulding paste and flatten to 6 mm/ $^{1}/_{4}$ in wide and 4.5 cm/$1^{3}/_{4}$ in long. Cut to a sharp point and slightly curve back from a deep mid rib. The backs of the leaves are coloured pale grey while the front is a shiny deep olive green.

MOUNTAIN DEVIL— SEED POD

Hook a length of medium gauge wire. Using moulding paste make a crescent shape on one end of the wire. Groove and cut down the centre on the top side. Open out to shape very pointed ears. Slightly point the other end to form the head. The devil is always brownish grey surrounded by leaves. A red devil made from moulding paste is added at one end of this plaque.

The brilliant red and the abundance of foliage of the mountain devil make it a striking centrepiece.

CONEBUSH

Jean Palmer

onebush, commonly called pixie mop, is a member of the protea family. It grows through most of Australia and comes in subtle shades of pinks, greys and greens.

CLOSED FLOWER

Take a small pea-sized ball of moulding paste and shape into a long slim bud with a small bulb on top. Mark the bulb with four lines to represent the petals. The finished bud should be 2.5 cm/1 in long. Make approximately twenty-seven of these closed flowers.

OPEN FLOWER

Take a small pea-sized ball of moulding paste and make a narrow cone 2.5 cm/1 in long and 2 mm/1/8 in across the top. Hollow out to a depth 1.25 cm/1/2 in, keeping the opening slim. Cut four petals and round off the top of each. Thin out each petal and vein with a pin. Turn the petals well back and insert one fine red stiffened cotton stamen that is tipped with yellow runny royal icing. Allow to dry thoroughly.

When all the pieces are dry, colour a pale rose pink mixed with alcohol. Allow to dry then dust the bulb with mid-grey chalk, coat lightly with egg white and roll in gelatine. Allow to dry.

ASSEMBLY

Group all pieces into a star-burst arrangement including three to five of the dry open flowers and tape the stem.

CALYX

Take a large pea-sized ball of green moulding paste and hollow out slightly. Using sharp scissors, cut markings in

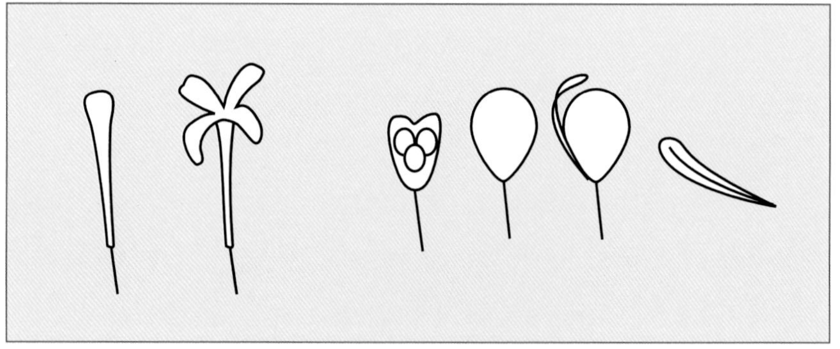

Patterns for the flower, calyx and bud.

the calyx as shown. Dampen the base of the flower and insert the calyx into the stem pulling it up to the base. Repair the markings where necessary. When dry paint the calyx with a medium blue/green colour and touch the tops of the cuts with brown to highlight.

BUD

Using moulding paste, make a fat tear drop approximately 1.25 cm/½ in long and 6 mm/¼ in wide and insert a strong wire into the pointed end. Allow to dry. Using moulding paste make small cones which are flattened and curved on top. Attach to the dried centre. Curve the cones towards the centre alternating the pieces in approximately three rows—twenty-seven pieces. When dry, colour as before. The calyx is the same as the flower.

LEAVES

Take a small log of green moulding paste and insert a dampened unhooked wire. Flatten the piece and roll to approximately 2.5 cm/1 in long and 7.5 cm/3 in wide. Round the tip and taper a slim base around the wire.

Tape the leaves together with the flowers and buds and secure to the cake with a little royal icing.

Conebush are tiny flowers and are ideal mixed with larger flowers and ribbons. *(See page 175.)*

PITTOSPORUM

Donna Baldock

hese shrubs and trees grow in Asia, Australia, parts of California and Africa. Some species grow in moist rainforest and one species grows in the dry, inland areas of Australia. It is often called native daphne. The flowers are white with caramel centres and the seed pods are plump cushions bulging with red seeds.

SEED PODS

Make the seeds by rolling tiny red balls of moulding paste. Prepare a batch of mustard coloured moulding paste and roll into a tube 2.5 cm/1 in long and 1.25 cm/$^1/_2$ in thick. Hollow out deeply with a modelling tool and make long cuts down each side to make two halves. Snip and round off the top edges and thin out each side until about 8 mm/$^1/_3$ in wide. Smooth the edges and pinch the tips. Thread thick brown-covered wire through the base and secure.

Paint the inside of the prepared pod with a gum arabic solution/edible glue and line liberally with the tiny red seeds in staggered lines. Paint over the seeds again with gum arabic solution as in the wild these are covered with a clear sticky substance.

Make a groove from the bottom of the cut on each side to indicate the seed pods will open further. When dry, paint small brown streaks on the back of the pod, then paint over with clear water to blur the brown streaks.

LEAVES

The leaves are about twice the length of the seed pod and as wide as the pods are long. They are shiny and stiff with lightly fluted edges but no serrations with the sides folded out from a central vein. The leaves are mid to dark green, shiny on top and paler and dull on the back. Cut these from moulding paste and when dry colour as shown.

FLOWER

Prepare the centre by taping a pale blue/green tipped white stigma onto a white covered wire. Dip some white headless stamens 1.25 cm/$^1/_2$ in long in egg white and then fine lemon jelly crystals or precoloured fine semolina.

Take a pea-sized piece of moulding paste and make a flat-headed cone. Hollow out with a modelling tool. Make five deep cuts and finger pull each petal. Do not clip the edges of the petals. Thin out with a stick or tool and fold the petals right back.

Slightly dampen the centre of the flower and place a prepared stamen between each petal. Press into place so that it stands up straight. Tip each stamen into very diluted caramel brown liquid colour. Moisten the end of a stigma wire and insert in the centre of the flower.

CALYX

The calyx is very fine, pale greeny brown and folded back.

The unusual seed pod of the pittosporum develops into small white flowers.

SCAEVOLA

Donna Baldock

hese purple flowers are often called fan flowers because the petals form a hand shape or fan. There are some sixty-nine varieties of scaevola (*Ramosissima*) found in Australia alone. It is named after Scaevola, the Roman soldier who is said to have shown his great courage by burning off his hand in a fire.

CENTRE

Shape a tiny piece of moulding paste in to a teardrop and place on a hooked wire. Flatten out thinly and, with a pin, shred around the edge and roll with a modelling tool to thin further. Slightly cup the centre then fold back at the tip.

FLOWER

Form a pea-sized piece of moulding paste into a cone and hollow out to a length of approximately 2 cm/$^{3}/_{4}$ in. Cut a very deep V in the side of the cone. It should be about half the length of the cone. Thin out the remainder and make five even cuts for the petals. Clip the corners of each petal.

Using a modelling tool, thin the edges of the petals leaving a thicker V through the centre with the point towards the tip of the petal. Carefully ruffle the thinned part of the petal making sure it has a nice rounded shape. Spread the petals so they are in the shape of a fan and lightly curve back.

Moisten very sparingly in the centre of the flower and insert the prepared centre piece, pressing towards the cut-out piece of the cone so that the backward fold is towards the outside of the flower leaving a distinct hollow in the centre of the petals.

Colour the petals in a mauve/lilac shade. The centre is coloured pale yellow. The back of the insert is reddish brown with the tip left white. The sides of the cut-out are coloured greyish-brown. The calyx is tiny and green, curling down away from the flower.

The leaves are approximately 2.5 cm/1 in long and 1.25 cm /$^{1}/_{2}$ in wide. They have no serrations and are a long oval shape with a faint main vein but no side veins. They are coloured mid-green with a faint red edging.

This unusual flower has five petals on one side of the centre.

MAGNOLIA

Carol Wright

agnolias are large creamy/pink flowers which grow on big trees with very little foliage at flowering time. They have a superb perfume and are difficult to propagate. Because of this they are expensive to buy and often hard to find. They are a favourite flower with brides the world over.

CENTRE

Take a small pea-sized ball of moulding paste and push onto a hooked wire. Roll between the fingers to form a sausage-shaped cone with a pointed end. Use small sharp scissors to snip all over the cone. Allow to dry and then paint a pale green.

FLOWER STAMENS

The stamens are made from thick cotton. Wrap two lengths of cotton thread, cream and burgundy, around your finger at least thirty times. Thread a wire through the cotton and twist at the base. Next cut the cotton to the required length and feed the dry centre down through the cotton stamens and tape together. Do not cut the wires to thin out because the magnolia does have a rather thick stem.

Large Petal   Small Petal   Leaf   Centre   Bud

Patterns for the petals, leaf, centre and bud.

PETALS

The flower has nine petals—six small and three slightly larger. Using the patterns, cut the petals from very thin moulding paste. Attach each petal to a wire and using a balling tool, curve the petals according to the shaded area shown on the patterns. Allow to dry

thoroughly and then colour the backs of the petals only.

Arrange the first three small petals evenly around the taped centre. Place the next three large petals in the spaces between the first petals. Secure and tape together. Finally use tape to secure the last three small petals in the centre.

CALYX

Using a cone-shaped piece of moulding paste feed onto the wire at the back of the flower. Paint with egg white and press onto the back of the last layer of flower petals.

Cut a second shape according to the pattern and curl slightly backwards like a rosehip. Glaze the back of the calyx and roll in finely shredded cotton wool which is precoloured a browny/green. Allow to dry and secure to the back of the inside calyx with egg white.

BUD

Take a marble-sized piece of moulding paste and feed onto a hooked wire. Shape into a large tear drop shape. Roll between the fingers to form a point at the top. Paint the bud with glaze and roll in finely shredded cotton wool which is precoloured in a browny/green. Allow to dry.

Take a small pea-sized piece of moulding paste, shape into a cone and feed onto the back of the bud. Secure with egg white and brown tape.

LEAVES

Using the pattern, cut the leaves from very thin moulding paste and secure to wire. Allow to dry and colour in a deep green with the edges fading off to a lighter shade. The leaves are wired separately to the flower and are used sparingly.

To achieve such fine petals, the moulding paste must be rolled very thinly.

CLEMATIS

Rosemary Bruce-Mullins

lematis is an Australian native and is a member of the ranunculi family. It is a vigorous climber with its tendrils twining their way throughout the bush and on many fences. It grows in the dry woodlands throughout temperate areas of Australia.

CENTRES

Using white cotton thread, wrap around two fingers sixty times. Tie off each end with green wire and cut the cotton threads in half. Securely tape the wires and trim to approximately 1.25 cm/½ in. Dampen the top of the cottons with gum glue and dab in cornmeal/polenta or yellow chalk powder. If you prefer you can use purchased stamens.

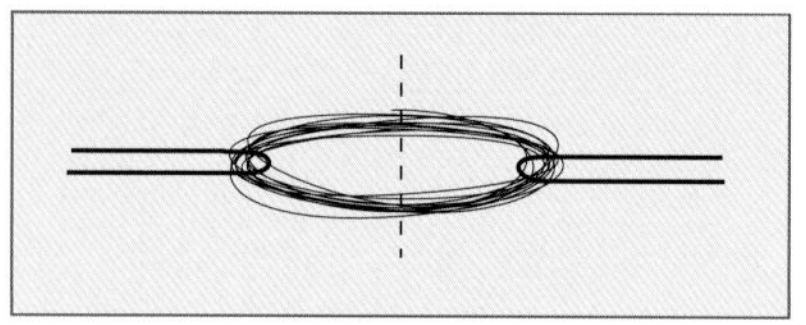

Cutting line for cotton thread.

BUDS

Closed bud: Attach an oval ball of moulding paste to a hooked wire. Mark the sides of the ball to represent petals about to open. Paint around the join with runny royal icing to form the calyx. Leave to dry. When dry colour with violet chalk and steam.

Open bud: Using a rose petal cutter, cut four petals. Vein the outside and ball each petal so that it curves. Dampen the side of each petal and join together to form a cup. Place a prepared centre in the middle and finger the bottom of the cupped petals so that they adhere to the wire. Paint runny royal icing around the join to form the calyx and allow to dry. When dry, lightly chalk the outside of all the petals with violet chalk. The base of the flower should have a little more colour. Steam gently to give a shine.

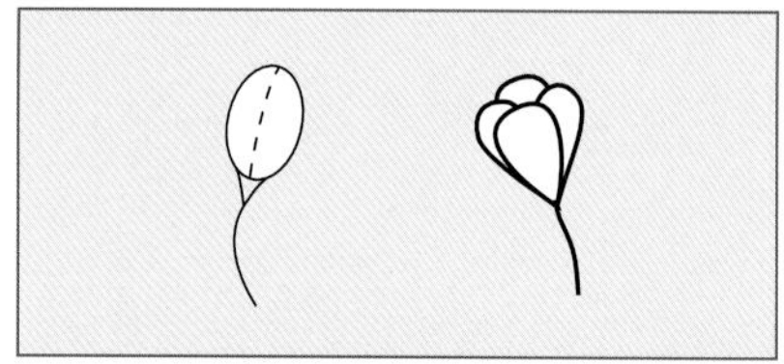

Patterns for closed and open buds.

FLOWER

Cut out four petals for each flower, neaten the edges and vein. Press a balling tool into the back of each petal and join to form a cross. Dampen the base of the centre with gum paste and push through the centre of the petals. Use foil to shape if necessary then leave to dry. When dry brush very lightly with violet chalk. Paint runny royal icing around the

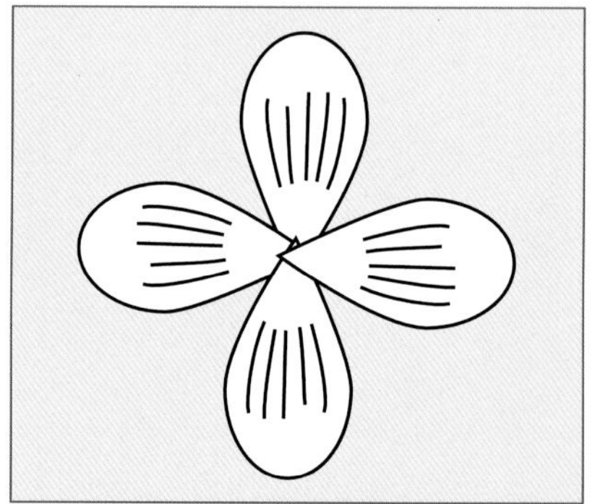

Pattern for flower.

base to form the calyx and strengthen the join.

LEAVES

Roll out green moulding paste leaving it a little thicker in the centre at the base. Use the patterns to cut out the leaf shapes. Neaten the edges and insert a wire into the thickened area. Vein the leaf and press with fingers to secure the wire. Make sure that the middle is still sufficiently thick to ensure the wire does not come through the paste. Finish shaping the leaf and allow to dry. Dust the leaf all over with

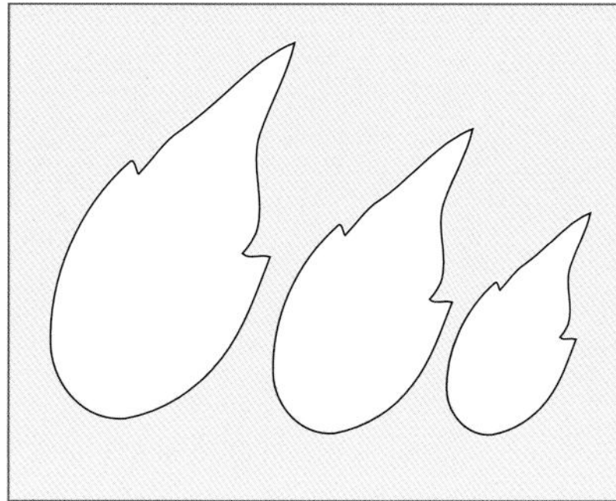

Patterns for three leaf sizes.

green chalk and shade the centres with burgundy.

STEAMING

When all pieces have been dusted with chalk, steam them over rapidly boiling water so that the petal dusts are absorbed into the paste to increase the shine and give a more natural look.

ASSEMBLY

Tape the leaves together in sets of three with two smaller leaves flanking a larger leaf.

Tape the pieces together in the following order—one set of small leaves, a closed bud, one set of small leaves, an open bud, one set of small leaves, one flower, one set of large leaves, one flower, one set of large leaves, one flower, one set of large leaves.

Step-by-step technique for the assembly of a sprig of clematis.

WATTLE

Rosemary Bruce-Mullins

cacia myrtifolia, or wattle as it is more commonly known, grows thoughout Australia and is probably the most recognised and popular Australian native. The flowers are actually small balls of yellow fluff with no petals.

BUDS

Tape together four or five stamens to form each bud. Tape these stamens to a piece of fine green wire. Paint some of the stamen heads in a pale yellow colour with a dash of brown. Allow to dry.

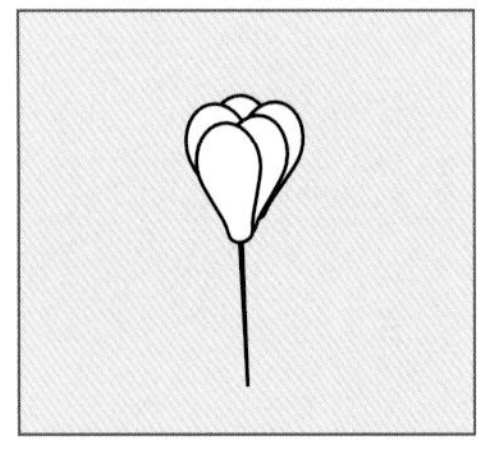

Pattern for bud.

LEAVES

Colour a batch of moulding paste to a dark green. Using a small leaf cutter, cut the leaves from the paste and insert a wire in one end of each leaf. Mark the leaves with a veiner that has a heavy central vein and light side veins. Gently shape them and allow to dry. The leaves of wattle are generally the same size along the stem.

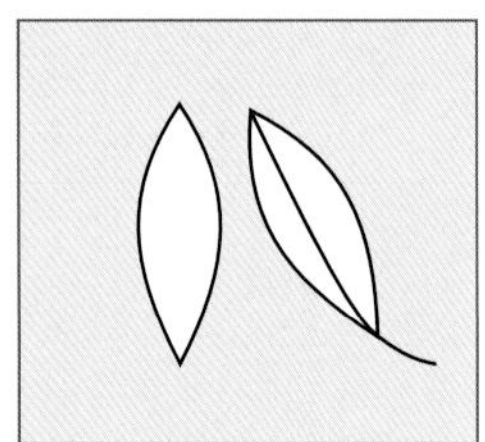

Pattern for leaves.

FLOWERS

Put a small pea-sized piece of moulding paste on fine green wire to form the flower centre. Allow to dry. When dry moisten the ball with gum paste or egg white and then roll gently in cornmeal/polenta until fully covered. It is best to put the cornmeal/polenta into a shallow container to make rolling easier. When completed the whole thing must be covered to resemble a fluffy yellow ball.

Pattern for flower.

ASSEMBLY

Tape the flowers, buds and leaves together on a single stem. The leaves are placed in pairs along the stem with buds and flowers mixed together as the stem goes along.

Step-by-step pieces for making a sprig of wattle.

JASMINE

Rosemary Bruce-Mullins

he perfume of jasmine on a warm summer's night is hard to forget. A native of China this delicate climber brings romance and fantasy to any cake. It can be used alone or as a trailing piece in a bouquet of larger flowers.

LEAVES

Using green moulding paste cut out leaves of three different sizes. Work the edges with your fingers to remove the cut look. Mark using a veiner with a heavy central vein and light side veins. Shape the leaves into a V shape and leave to dry. When dry dust with dark green chalk and steam to shine.

Patterns for leaves.

BUDS

Using fine green wire and white moulding paste, work a small amount of paste onto a wire. The stem of the bud should be approximately 2.5 cm/1 in long and the bud is formed as a bulb on the top of the stem. Leave to dry. When dry dust with pink petal dust and steam.

Patterns for buds.

FLOWERS

Form the stems of the flowers by working a small amount of moulding paste along a wire to a length of 2.5 cm/1 in. Make sure the length of paste extends beyond the end of the wire. Cut the end of the paste bluntly to a length of 1.25-2 cm/$^{1}/_{2}$-$^{3}/_{4}$ in for the flower stem. Form the flower top by rolling white moulding paste out thinly. Cut out the flower with a small five-petal calyx cutter. Ball each petal of the flower quite heavily to give the points a rounded shape and curve the petals back towards

Patterns for flowers.

the stem. Dampen the blunt cut end of the flower stem and stick to the centre of the formed flower. Turn the flower right side up and make a hole with a pointed tool. Insert the end of a yellow stamen in this hole and set aside to dry. When dry dust the stem and the back of the flower with pink petal dust and steam. Allow to dry thoroughly before assembling the sprays.

ASSEMBLY

When all the pieces are dry, cover all the wires with green tape. When taping the stems of the buds and flowers start the tape just on the base of the icing so that it appears as if the buds are coming out from the stems. Wire the leaves together in sprays of five with a large leaf at the top, two medium leaves next and then finally the two small leaves.

FLOWER AND BUD SPRAY

Tape the flowers and buds together in sprays with odd numbers of flowers and buds. To complete the spray, the flowers and leaves are taped together so that the sprays of flowers come out of the joining of a pair of leaves. Continue in this way all along the stem using the larger leaves at the tip of the stem.

Step-by-step pieces for making a spray of jasmine.

PROTEA

Kath Swansbra

his is a heavy flower with waxy petals and leaves. It originally came from South Africa but now grows well in many countries with similar climates such as south-western United States and most of Australia. It requires a strong wire stem to hold the weight of the finished flower.

CENTRE SUPPORT

Tape a piece of heavy florist's wire approximately 10 cm/4 in long or use four pieces of heavy cake decorating wire. Hook the end and mould a large piece of moulding paste into an egg shape. Dampen the hooked end of the wire and mould the paste firmly around it. It should resemble a small egg. Pierce all over with a fine needle and allow to dry out for several days.

CENTRE AND STAMENS

Using a no. 0 piping tube and medium peak royal icing, pipe lines from the base of the centre support to the top. Allow to dry and then pipe two more layers. When dry attach the extra stamens made from moulding paste. Roll small pieces of moulding paste into long log shapes, dampen the bases and stick to the base of the centre support. The height of the paste stamens is the same length as the piped stamens. Allow to dry and then colour. Dampen the tips of the stamens with egg white or icing glue and then dip them into fine semolina.

PETALS

Thinly roll out moulding paste and, using a set of three water-lily cutters, cut twelve petals of each size. Place each petal on a

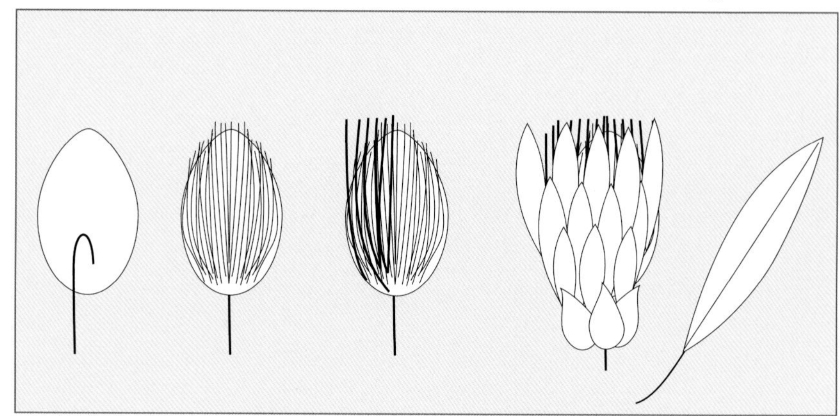

Patterns for the centre flower and leaf.

piece of foam and vein down the centre with a veining tool. Pinch the top of each petal and keep the base area flat. Allow to dry thoroughly and then colour as illustrated.

Use a small rose petal cutter and cut ten to twelve petals. Hollow and shape the centre with a balling tool. Allow to dry and colour.

The exact number of petals on each flower depends on the size of the centre.

ASSEMBLY

Use royal icing and a no. 1 piping tube to join the petals to the flower centre. Begin with the largest petals and place them so that the tips of the petals are 2 mm/$^{1}/_{8}$ in above the flower centre and are evenly spaced around the centre. When the first row has dried and set, place the medium petals lower and in between the first row. Allow to dry then add the smaller petals alternate to the previous row. Place the rose petal shapes at the base.

LEAVES

Shape some moulding paste into a log and insert a fine wire. Roll out finely and cut out some leaves. You can do this freehand or use a long thin leaf cutter such as poinsettia. Keep the tip rounded, vein down the centre and curve. Colour when dry. Make six or seven leaves and tape around the flower.

Proteas are very large strong flowers with no perfume.

NATIVE ORCHID

Linda McGlinn

s soon as I was introduced to the spindly splendour of the tiny Australian native orchid, *Dendrobium teretifolium* or rat tail orchid I realised that this delicate little Aussie was ideal for use on cakes. It also provides a challenge for sugar artists because the petals are extremely long and narrow and can easily break.

FLOWERS

Begin by forming a very tiny column of moulding paste on a length of fine wire. Allow to dry. Roll the paste finely and cut a throat, frill the lower edge and roll under.

Cut one petal A and make a small cut in the base of the petal to take the wire. Attach to the outside edge of the column, turn backwards. Allow to dry and then colour.

Cut two B petals and attach one to either side of throat. Allow to dry and then colour.

Cut two C petals and attach over the top of the previous petals and turn back. Allow to dry and then colour.

The flowers are attached to the fine spindly stems that should curve at different angles. Add a length of soft green ribbon to finish the display. These tiny orchids can be displayed as the main decoration, as part of a bouquet or arranged on a sugar plaque. They add lightness to any design.

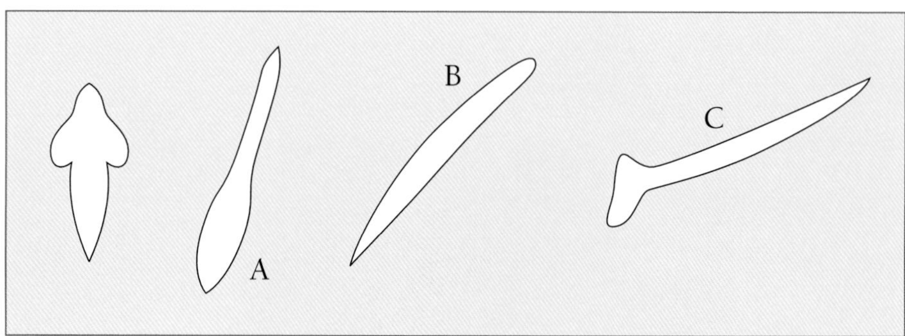

Patterns for the centre and different-sized petals.

This arrangement is designed to display these tiny flowers at their best. *(See page 181.)*

WATERLILY

Kath Swansbra

lthough waterlilies are seldom used in cake decorating this cake had to be completed without the use of wires or supports. Waterlilies were ideal for this purpose because I was able to float them on the pond.

STAMENS

Roll out small pieces of moulding paste into thin logs about 1.25 cm/$^{1}/_{2}$ in long. Dampen the tip with icing glue and dip into coloured semolina. Allow to dry.

PETALS

Use three different-sized waterlily cutters to cut and shape ten to twelve petals of each size. Lay each petal on foam and mark the centre with a veining tool. Allow to dry then colour.

ASSEMBLY

Use a deep patty cake pan or similar to support the flowers. Place a large pea-sized piece of moulding paste in the centre of a 2.5 cm/1 in square of aluminium foil and flatten. Place one piece for each flower into one recess in the pan.

Place the large petals into the paste with a little royal icing. Next place the middle-sized petals into position alternating with the first row then place the small petals into position alternating with the previous row.

Pipe a little royal icing in the centre and push the dried stamens into the centre until the royal icing is no longer visible. Use small pieces of

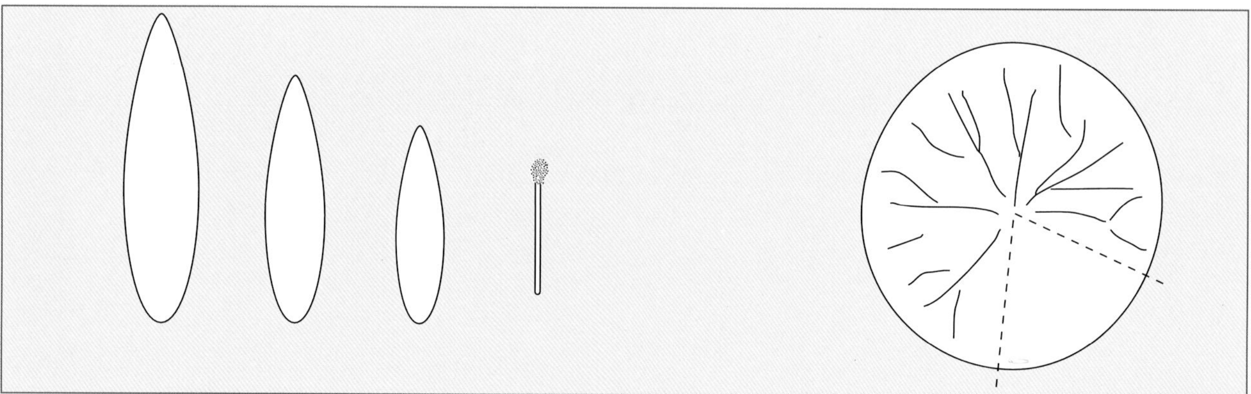

Patterns for petals and leaf.

foam or cotton wool to keep the petals in their correct positions until the flower has set and is completely dry.

LEAF

Using moulding paste, cut out a few different-sized circles. Frill the edges and shape according to the pattern. Mark with a veining tool and cut out a small V section. Allow to dry then colour a dull green colour and paint with edible shine.

ROCKS

The rocks for this cake also had to be made with no support and had to be light so that I could place them around the waterfall and the church.

First select some real stones in the shapes that you require. Wash them thoroughly and leave to dry. Roll out a quantity of moulding paste and place over the real rocks to get the shape. Allow to dry out just a little. When partially dry, carefully remove the paste from around the rocks, reshape and prop with foam or cotton wool until completely dry.

Roll out pieces of moulding paste into long logs and attach to the inside base of the rocks to form an edge. Brush the rocks with a thin covering of royal icing. Colour when dry.

For moss or lichen-covered rocks make a stiff batch of green royal icing and dab onto the rocks with a brush.

These waterlilies and rocks are made without wires or support. All parts are edible. *(See page 169.)*

SPIDER CHRYSANTHEMUM

Kath Swansbra

hrysanthemums originally came from Japan and China and are still a symbol of Japanese flora. There are hundreds of varieties ranging from bulbous strong flowers to daisies. This variety has spindly petals and looks great mixed in an arrangement of roses.

CENTRE

Mould a pea-sized piece of moulding paste over a piece of medium-weight wire and allow to dry thoroughly. This is the centrepiece. Roll out moulding paste thinly and cut out two sets of petals with the smallest chrysanthemum cutter. Cut each petal in half and curl each one with a veining tool.

Dampen the centrepiece and thread through the centre of the petals. Ease up the petals close around the centrepiece base. Attach a second set of petals alternately with the first set. Allow to dry.

Take some small pieces of moulding paste and roll into thin logs. Dampen the base of the log and attach to the base of the centrepiece. Curve the tip in over the top. Continue until the centre looks full.

Roll slightly larger pieces of moulding paste into logs, dampen and stick to the base but allow the tips to curve away from the centre.

OUTER PETALS

Roll moulding paste into a log and insert a piece of dampened extra fine wire. Roll between your hands until thin. Flatten the tip and mark it with a wooden toothpick or cocktail stick to resemble a hollow petal. Make at least fifty of these petals ranging in length from 2 cm/$^3/_4$ in to 3.75 cm/ 1$^1/_2$ in—some curved and some straight. Tape the petals around the centre until the flower looks very full and spidery.

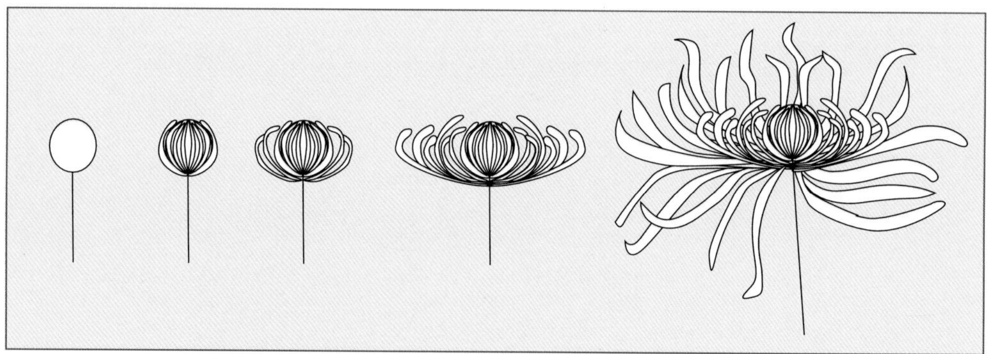

Pattern and positioning of centre and petals.

Spider chrysanthemums make a truly striking display on a wedding cake. *(See page 173.)*

CYMBIDIUM ORCHID

Adèle Humphrys

ymbidium orchids are the traditional choice for a corsage. They are usually grown under glasshouse conditions and come in almost any colour imaginable. They keep well under refrigeration and therefore turn up in floral arrangements all over the world.

COLUMN

Take a length of hooked wire and attach a small ball of moulding paste. Push down the wire a little to form a bulb. The length and width of the centre column will depend on the size of the orchid you wish to make. Allow to dry and colour in deep rose. Add two small dots of royal icing to complete the column.

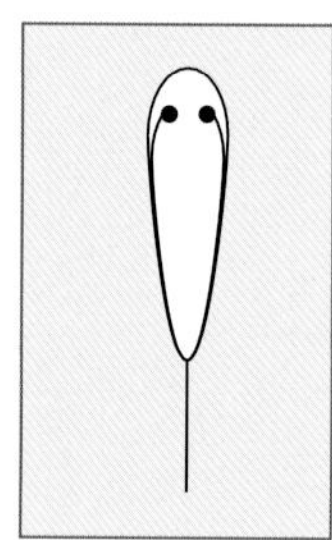

Pattern for column.

THROAT

Roll out some moulding paste and cut out the throat according to the pattern. Shade the base in deep rose and then vein. Add two fine lines as shown using tweezers or any suitable tool. Thin all the edges of the throat but do not frill. Attach to the column and the base and curve away from the throat. Place on foam or cotton wool to dry thoroughly. When dry apply colour in small splotches over the body of the throat. Stroke colour around the edges.

Pattern for throat.

PETALS

Using moulding paste, cut five petals according to the pattern. Lightly vein each petal and

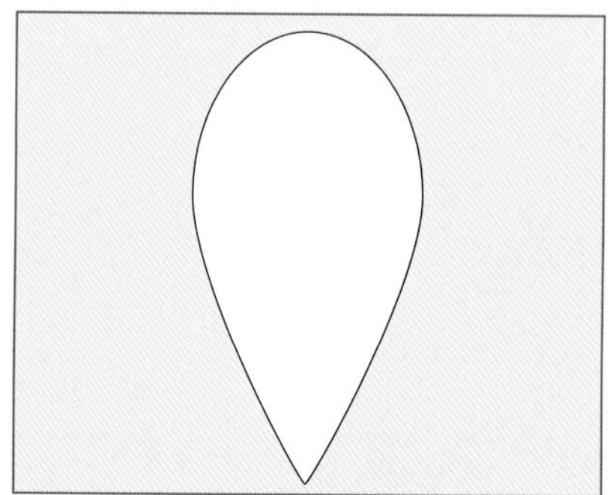

Pattern for petal.

attach to a length of fine gauge wire. For each flower, place two (A) petals on their backs over a curved surface and place two (B) petals face down over the same curve to dry and allow the fifth (C) petal to dry naturally.

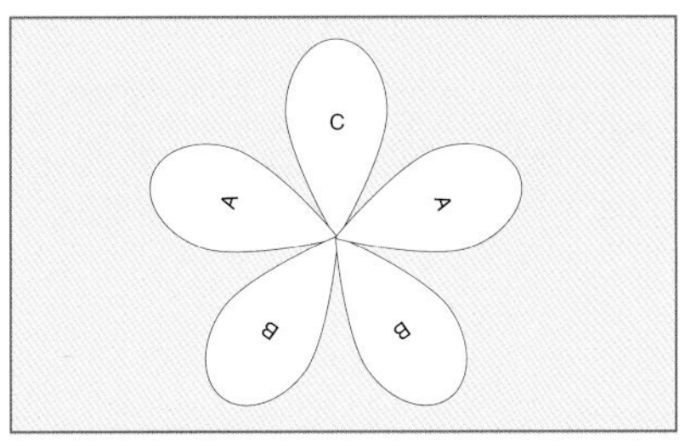

Pattern for flower assembly.

ASSEMBLY

Following the pattern, tape together the two concave petals with the natural shape petal and then insert the two backwards petals. Insert the throat into the centre and adjust the final positions.

Intricate hand painting of the throat is the secret of a life-like cymbidium orchid. *(See page 179.)*

SWEET PEA FLOWER

Carol Wright

weet peas are soft delicate flowers with curly tendrils that attach to almost anything. They grow just about anywhere in the world in all the soft pastel shades that delight cake decorators.

FLOWER

Cut a 20 cm/8 in length of wire. Bend to form a stalk. Take a small piece of moulding paste and thread onto the wire and roll to form a sausage shape. Place 1.25 cm/$^{1}/_{2}$ in silk stamen in the end.

Roll out a batch of moulding paste thinly. Using the pattern cut two bud shapes. Thin the edges and run a balling tool up the centre. Place on each side of the wired centre and press front edges together. Secure the bottom edges onto the wire.

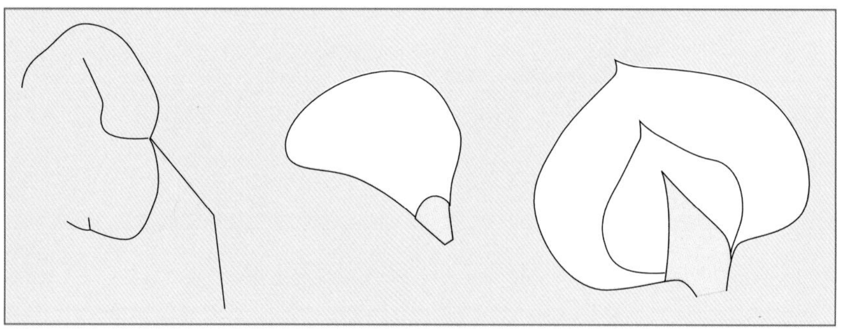

Patterns for the tendril and flower.

Cut two wing petals from moulding paste and run a small ball tool down the back of each petal. Thin and flute the front of each petal. Attach these two halves with egg white on either side of the bud at the bottom.

Using moulding paste cut the back petal. Thin the edges with a balling tool and flute. Turn over and pinch the centre of the back to form an indentation in the front. Brush with egg white and press and fold onto the bud. Fold the top half of the back petal backwards to give a natural appearance.

CALYX

Use a small ball of moulding paste and make a small Mexican hat shape and cut out a small star shape. Moisten with egg white and push onto the wired dry sweet pea flower. Neaten the back by rolling between your fingers.

Pattern for calyx.

LEAVES

Use the pattern to cut the required number of leaves and wire them in pairs. Use very fine wire to make the tendrils.

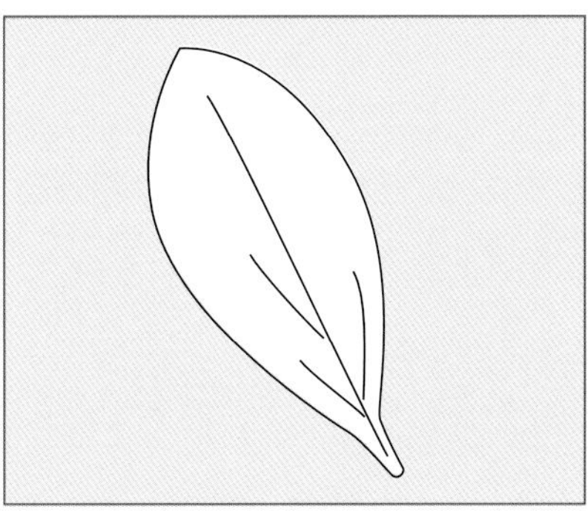

Pattern for leaf.

BUD

Make the buds shapes on wire as shown. Add one small back petal and close around the bud. The buds are generally in groups of three.

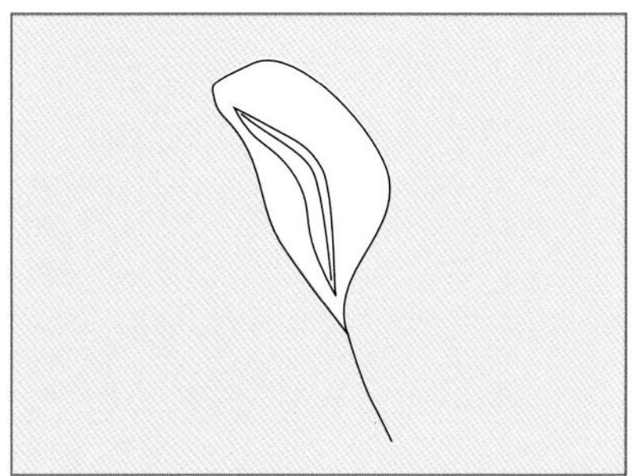

Pattern for bud.

Two tiny fairies are hiding in amongst the sweet peas. *(See page 171.)*

FLANNEL FLOWER

Eileen Scriven

lannel flowers have a daisy-like appearance with an off-white felt-like finish on their green-tipped petals. The foliage is an unusual green/grey shade. They are common in the eastern states of Australia.

CENTRE

Attach a medium-sized ball of cream moulding paste to a length of hooked wire. Allow to dry then paint with egg white and roll in a mix of semolina and green powder colour. Leave aside to dry again.

A flannel flower has ten petals on average and each petal is individually wired to make assembly easy.

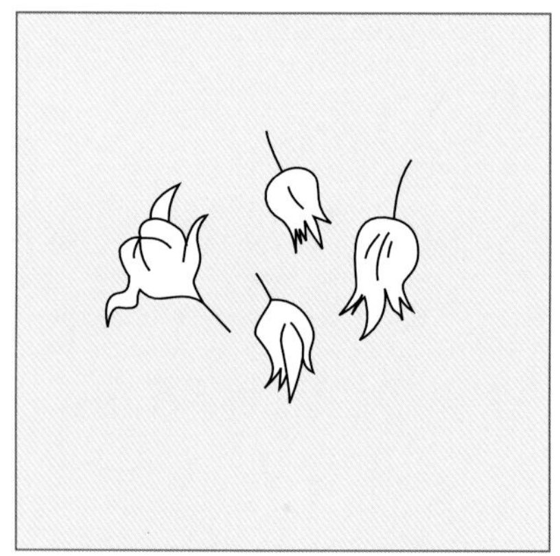

Patterns for centre.

PETAL

To a length of white medium gauge wire attach a small piece of cream moulding paste in a sausage shape. Roll out to a long thin shape.

Flatten a vein and press to thin the edges and top of the petal. Twist the tip slightly before colouring with green chalk. Allow to dry before assembling around the centre.

Pattern for flower.

LEAF

Colour a batch of moulding paste to a leaf green. Using medium gauge wire, attach some of the coloured paste and roll out to the size of the leaf pattern. Cut the leaf, vein and allow to dry. When dry the leaf is given the natural felt-like effect by gently dipping it in a mixture of grey powder food colour and gelatine.

Patterns for leaves.

Flannel flowers have felt-like petals with a slate green soft centre. *(See page 185.)*

FREESIA

Lynette Speer

reesias are known for their unique fragrance and now with the amazing variety of hybrids available it is possible to have them in flower most of the year. They are a dainty flower and are used frequently in cake decorating.

FLOWER

Flatten the end of one stamen cotton then using a scalpel, slit the end into three or four parts. Tape the stamen cotton to three stamens keeping it slightly above the stamens.

Form a rather large ball of moulding paste into a Mexican hat and cut out the flower shape from this with a daffodil cutter. Soften the petal edges with a balling tool and vein with a corn husk. Rest the petals over the edge of a foam pad and gently press the balling tool into the widest section of each petal. Lightly run the balling tool from the tip to the centre to curl the edges of the petals inwards.

Use a modelling tool to hollow out the centre of the flower to form a long trumpet. Do not make it too wide. Dampen the end of the prepared bunch of stamens and insert them into the trumpet. Pull them through the base until the stamens are below the tips of the petals. Roll the base between fingers to smooth and shape. Hang upside down and allow to dry for a partially open flower. Stand upright to dry for a fully open flower.

Roll out moulding paste thinly and cut one flower using a small daffodil cutter. Cut into three separate petals, soften the edges, vein and ball each petal as before. Dampen the base and the lower sides and attach to the dried trumpet, placing it over the space between the petals and at the same height.

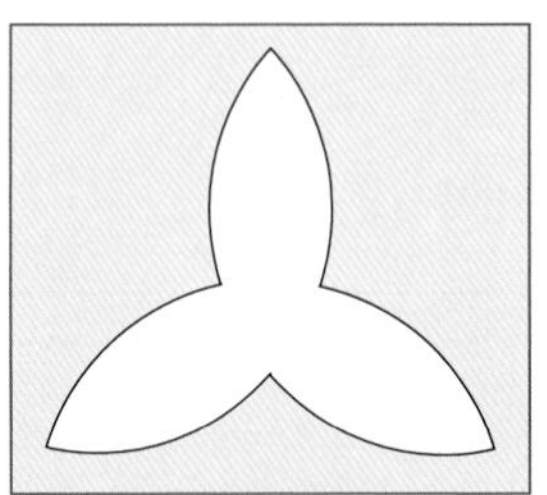

Pattern for flower.

CALYX

Make a small cone from green moulding paste. Cut through the centre at the top and approximately halfway to the base. Open it out slightly and cup the inside with a curling pin. Thread onto the flower

wire and secure at the base of the flower. Allow to dry.

BUDS

The buds are elongated and set into a two-petal calyx the same as the flower.

LEAVES

The leaves are straplike with lengthwise veining.

COLOURING

Freesias come in variety of main colours but there are a few standards to follow. Paint the inside of the throat a deep yellow. The tips of the stamens, the top one-third of the inside of the petals and the whole of the outside are painted to match the colour of the flower. The base near the calyx is always coloured yellow.

ASSEMBLY

Tape a small bud together with a number of the medium buds and the flowers to form a spike. Attach these spikes and some leaves in single file but slightly offset along a stem.

Freesias are even-sized flowers that are ideal in groups or as fillers in bouquets. *(See page 177.)*

BANKSIA CONE

Jean Cole-Clark

hese strange looking banksia cones are the seed pods of the banksia plant. They are a native of Australia and come in many different shapes and sizes. They grow on a strong thick stem attached to a leafy branch and the individual pods break open after a bush fire and spread their seed to rejuvenate the bush.

BASE

Because the weight of the moulding paste is very heavy, it is necessary to form the centre of such a large piece from pastillage which is much lighter. Shape a piece of pastillage into a large oval cone and push a wooden skewer into the centre. Leave to dry for twenty-four hours.

Colour a batch of moulding paste to a mid-grey and shape around the pastillage cone as shown. Smooth the joins. While the moulding paste is moist and using the end of a no. 3 or 4 piping tube, press small circles all over the surface of the cone. These should be close together and uneven. Do this while the moulding paste is still moist or it will crack.

Using a knife, cut some slots approximately 10 cm/4 in wide and 2.5 cm/1 in deep into the cone. These should be random and be the full length of the cone. Open each cut out into a V. Roll out some moulding paste thinly and cut into small ovals. Fold each one in half and push deeply into each slot. They should protrude from the surface of the cone as shown. Allow to dry.

When dry, paint the V pieces in dark brown/black. Paint all over the small circles in a lighter tone to resemble the natural banksia. Cover the stem in brown tape.

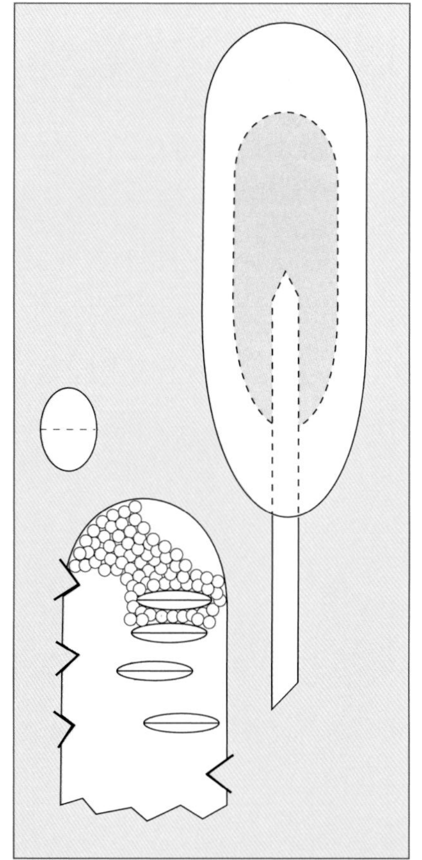

Patterns for base, cone and seed casing.

Banksia cones are large woody pods that pop open in bush fires. *(See page 95.)*

SECTION SIX

CELEBRATION CAKES

WEDDING

CHRISTENING

FANTASY

Flowers • Fairies • Drapes

RHAPSODY

Kath Swansbra

his lavish wedding cake was designed to suit the entry requirements for the 9th FHA International Salon Culinaire held in Singapore. The category called for a three-tier wedding cake with all decorations to be completely edible. No wire or supports were allowed.

These rules proved very challenging because we are all accustomed to using manufactured items such as stamens and ribbons. As all participants had the same set of rules the real challenge was to think of something different—thus the two-tiers forming the waterfall and the lily pond as the third tier.

Nature is very beautiful but proved not so easy to reproduce in sugar. The waterlilies were an ideal choice because they could be floated on the pond and did not need wires to support them.

It took some experimentation to perfect the natural look of the rocks and mosses. The rock formations are hollow, made from moulding paste then brushed over with thin royal icing. The caves behind the waterfall are filled with rocks, leaves and flowers. The whole piece is topped off with a fine filigree church complete with stained glass window and wedding rings inside.

The completed piece shows to full advantage the skills of an experienced decorator. Rhapsody is an imposing piece of sugar artistry. It won the gold medal at the 9th FHA International Salon Culinaire.

The three tiers are perfectly coordinated to form a prize-winning design. *(See pages 38, 46, 124 and 152.)*

FAIRY FANTASY

Carol Wright

airies are always a delight and lend themselves perfectly to cake decorating. Sweet peas are my favourite flowers and one day I realised that they resemble tiny fairy wings. With this idea in mind I drew the design for this cake.

The cake is covered with fondant and the side is decorated with brush floodwork in a pattern of sweet peas similar to those on the top. Fine extension work in deep scallops has then been added and piped lace completes the delicate effect of fairies and magic.

The exact arrangement of sweet peas and hidden flower fairies just seems to develop as you make the flowers. The different way they lie and the various twists of the tendrils establish the way the top is arranged. The fairies are flooded in a back-to-back method with sweet pea petals as skirts and wings and even the tiny hat on the small fairy. Their faces are peeping out from under the flowers.

The colour of the board is chosen to blend with the floral arrangement not detract from it. It is a dusty green raw silk which matches the green of the leaves rather than the usual idea of blending with the flower colours.

This cake was a pleasure to create and well worth the effort. It won first prize in the Queensland Show.

Delicate fairies hidden in the sweet peas add a whimsical feel to this christening cake. (See pages 10, 12 and 158.)

FOREVER

Kath Swansbra

ake decorators are often asked for a wedding cake design that is simple and romantic without lavish adornment. This cake fills that ideal. It is two-tier—but can be made as one—it is not too large and is embellished with exquisite ribbon extension work, a bridal couple and a spray of blossoms for a keepsake.

The secret of this design is to keep to the same colour but use different shades. The cake is covered in ivory fondant and is placed on a board covered in the same colour. The delicate extension work is outlined with loops of cream satin ribbon.

The couple has been flooded separately and then placed in position. They too are made in soft shades of cream and ivory. The tiny top tier continues the ribbon extension work and flowers. Cream satin has been draped over the stand to frame the cake.

Finally, the floral spray is designed to link the two tiers without the use of columns. The spray can be made to match the bride's flowers but I have chosen a spider chrysanthemum as a central blossom and surrounded it with cream roses with deep green leaves to frame the bouquet. The dropped ribbon holding the final rose draws the eye to the bride and groom.

A perfect spray of sugar flowers is the focal point of this two tier wedding cake. (See pages 50 and 154.)

FANFARE

Jean Palmer

y inspiration for the design of this cake is a love of Australian wildflowers. Their soft colours seem appropriate to capture the wedding spirit. In particular, I wished to include the soft pink and grey tones of the Western Australian conebush.

This cake is comprised of three fan-shaped tiers. The two base tiers are the same size and are set side by side and the smaller top tier is set behind, raised on a stand and tilted forward slightly.

The boards are iced in ivory and have rolled edges. A soft green fabric is draped over the presentation board and stand. The cake covering is pale ivory with handkerchief extension work and guipure lace in the same colour. The extension work has been curved up on each scallop.

For the floral arrangements I chose pink and grey conebush, cream everlasting daisies, flannel flowers, cream Geraldton wax, pink painted lady pea flowers and blue-green gum leaves. All have been shaded in soft greys, pinks and greens with ribbon loops.

This type of design can be made with one, two or three tiers and is easy to transport and arrange.

Each board is covered in fondant to match the cake covering and the extension work is designed to highlight the scallops. *(See pages 54 and 134.)*

BEWITCHED

Lynette Speer

istinctly art deco in style this wedding cake is made without the usual extension work, ribbons and lace. Styled around the perfect sphere it features elegant drapes and small posies of freesias. It is a great choice for the bride who is after a cake of distinction.

The sphere cake is supported with a wooden skewer set in a large block of foam which makes it easier to cover. The cake is covered with fondant and patiently smoothed to produce a perfect ball.

The base cake is placed on a covered board and after piping a finishing edge around the base, the drape is prepared. It is made from fondant with a little glycerine added. The fondant is then stretched along its length over skewers. The drape is carefully placed on the cake and decorated with wedding rings and flowers.

The urn is made from moulding paste with a marble appearance. It is held in place with a large skewer. The floral sprays and rings are positioned next and left to dry. Finally the sphere is put into position on top of the urn.

The finished cake is then displayed on a special board and is truly a cake for today.

A perfect sphere balanced on a marble urn is just right for this single tier wedding cake draped in fondant. (See pages 98 and 162.)

DAYDREAMS

Adèle Humphrys

iligree and orchids adorn the sides of this large diamond-shaped cake. The focal point is a cornelli work tulle church with rose windows and a fine spire.

The cake is placed on a flooded board which is trimmed with ribbon to match those on the orchids. The orchids are made from moulding paste and left to dry. They are then hand coloured and wired in small sprays for each corner.

The filigree pieces are piped over the required shape and left to dry. They are attached to the cake with royal icing.

The church is the real challenge. A pattern is made first and then the different pieces are cut from cotton tulle. The tulle is stiffened and left to dry in the desired shapes. The windows on each side are held in position with a little royal icing. It is best to put these in before assembling the church. Join the roof to the gables with a little royal icing. Carefully attach the arches and finally the spire which is a cone of stiffened tulle.

When the church is assembled the whole thing is piped over with cornelli work making sure that all the tulle joins are covered. The edges of the tulle are finished with a tiny lace edge but they can be left raw if neat enough.

The cross, on the spire is attached after the whole thing is in place. It's probably a good idea to make a few of these in case of breakage on delivery.

Stiffened cotton tulle is the base for this church which is piped all over in cornelli work. *(See pages 114, 120 and 156.)*

TROPICAL PARADISE

Linda McGlinn

his cake was specially designed to feature the very delicate rat tail orchid. These flowers are very tiny and are lost if included in a bouquet of larger flowers. The oval shape allowed me to show the fine stems and elongated leaves of this delicate bush plant.

The colours on the cake are minimal to emphasise the delightful shades of the flower itself.

The cake is placed on a linen board and covered with pale cream icing. The fine embroidery is kept as simple as possible so that it adorns the cake but does not detract from the orchids.

The extension work is scalloped around the lower edge curving up on one side with a tiny bow at its peak. The actual piping in this large scallop is worked at an angle with very long threads in the bridgework. The remainder of the bridgework is piped in the traditional manner with drop threads. Fine lace has been piped around the top edge of the bridgework.

The finished product highlights the delicateness of the petals and stems of this very unusual sugar flower.

Very long drop threads piped at an angle are the central theme of this wedding cake. (See pages 48 and 150.)

FANTASIA

Marian Jones

his three tier cake is based on the croquembouche shape. I was looking for something unusual—a shape that was different to those readily available in cake tins. And so I thought why not make the cake inside the croquembouche tins?

Lining the tins was fiddly but the real difficulty was in constructing a special frame to hold the tins and prevent them tipping over in the oven. The actual baking times were a matter of trial and error but eventually the cakes were cooked to perfection.

Using a paper template I rolled out the marzipan, cut the shape then laid the cake into position on the piece and gently attached the marzipan. The same method was repeated with the fondant covering, working very quickly to erase the join. The base boards are covered with fondant then allowed to dry.

Once I decided on the cake style I searched for many weeks before I found the flowers that I wanted to complement the shape. The tiny native pea that grows wild in our country gave me the answers and the colour scheme. I love the shaded pinks in the peas and the brilliant shiny green leaves with their interesting shapes and overall trailing formation.

The base of each cake is finished with fondant drapes. The stands were specially made in perspex and the tiers can be arranged in any order.

The combination of the wild blossom and unusual shape is the secret of this striking wedding cake.

These cakes were cooked inside croquembouche tins then covered with fondant. The stands were specially made in perspex. *(See page 98.)*

BUSH WEDDING

Eileen Scriven

y love of the greens and greys of our native bush flowers made it easy to design this cake. The flannel flower is an off-white daisy-like flower with soft furry petals. It grows profusely all over the temperate parts of the Australian bush yet is not used very often in decorating.

The floating extension work I usually use is improved here with the incorporation of a ribbon method I had seen elsewhere. A fair bit of planning on paper is needed to work out the exact way to create this intricate work.

The side design is in two sections with the upper part featuring the flannel flower piped on tiny squares of tulle and suspended between triangular pieces of moulding paste. Each square is finished with emerald green ribbon.

The lower section continues the ribbon around the circumference of the built-out pieces and from this the bridge is floated. The smaller tier is a replica of the lower one and each is placed on a special stand that is covered with white satin.

The flannel flowers with the addition of the occasional teatree flower make the perfect arrangement for the top of each tier. The whole cake takes on a regal appearance when on display. It won first prize in its section at the Royal Easter Show in Sydney Australia.

A combination of brush embroidery and floodwork adorns the surface of this cake enhancing the floating extension work. *(See pages 36, 52 and 160.)*

MIDNIGHT PERFUME

Carol Wright

agnolias conjure up the warmth of the deep south and take us back to the days of large plantations and parties on warm summer evenings. It is this feeling that I have tried to create with the cake.

The cake is covered with white fondant and placed on a satin covered board. A paper pattern is made for the side design and then it is outlined on the cake. The floral design is created on the outside of the cake tin—it maintains the curve—using brush floodwork. When dry it is attached to the cake with a series of tiny dots of royal icing to suspend it just off the side.

The extension work is piped with a very fine piping tube and is finished off with lace pieces. The magnolias are large flowers with nine petals. These are made in advance and allowed to dry before colouring and wiring into groups of three. Additional buds and leaves are added to complete the spray which is suspended on a hook secured into the cake.

The design for the top tier is identical to the bottom tier although the pattern is adjusted to the smaller size.

The cake is displayed on a fabric-covered board. The flower is suspended on a long rod covered in fabric to match the board.

This cake was the champion in the Open Two-tier Wedding Cake Section at the Queensland Cake Decorators' Association Show.

An imposing presentation is the focal point of this wedding cake. The magnolia theme is continued around the sides. *(See pages 14 and 140.)*

FLIGHT OF BIRDS

Adèle Humphrys

his cake features every element for a romantic wedding—a fairytale horse and carriage, an exquisite display of cream and yellow orchids and featherlight tulle birds carrying a piped tulle horseshoe suspended over the whole cake. The side lace is made up of curved heart-shaped lace panels.

Tulle work is a favourite of mine and it enables me to create a feeling of lightness about the design. Cattleya orchids were my main choice of focal flowers and using native broom I was able to trail them over the lower cake.

The base board is specially cut to allow room for the horse and carriage which are also based on stiffened tulle with flooded wheels. They are very fragile and extremely difficult to transport.

The horseshoe shape is cut from stiffened cotton tulle with delicate embroidery and lacework. This beautifully light and fine piece complements the tulle birds suspended on the ribbons and gives the finishing touch to the cake.

This cake was a prize-winning entry at the Australian National Cake Competition.

This cake features a variety of different techniques including flooded lace, tulle work and royal piping.
(See pages 35, 116 and 117.)

WILD ROSE

Barbara Batterham

ometime ago I found a beautiful picture filled with wild roses. They were very delicately coloured that they were almost transparent. It was this picture that gave me the inspiration to create this design.

The petals of the roses are made from the palest cream moulding paste and wired together with a centre dipped in cornmeal/polenta. In an endeavour to achieve the transparency of the original picture every petal, rosehip and leaf is hand-painted. The wet look is achieved by mixing a little colour with liquid glucose and a drop of water. A small amount of this is brushed on the petals and then blended into the icing.

The bottom tier is sculptured to allow room for the spray to nestle in and give a line through to the pillar. The pillar is embroidered with wild roses in a three-dimensional back-to-back design. Part of each rose is created on the inside with the remainder on the outside of the pillar. The end result is that the pillar disappears and the roses seem to be suspended in mid-air.

The delicate embroidery and extension border complement the design and lend the final ethereal effect to a truly beautiful cake.

The embroidery on this pillar is worked inside and outside creating a three-dimensional effect. *(See pages 42 and 108.)*

SECTION SEVEN

RECIPES AND INDEX

ROYAL ICING

MOULDING PASTE

PASTILLAGE

Ingredients • Mixing • Storing

ROYAL ICING

Recipe no 1

1 egg white at room temperature

1¾ cups/280 g/9 oz pure icing/confectioner's sugar, well sifted

2 drops acetic acid or white vinegar, optional

Place the egg white in a glass bowl and beat gently to break up. Gradually add the sugar one spoonful at a time beating well after each addition. Keep adding the sugar until the mixture is the required consistency, then add the acetic acid or vinegar if using. Mix well and continue to add sugar until the mixture reaches the required consistency.

Recipe no 2

1 teaspoon/½ oz egg white powder/actiwhite/merriwhite

⅓ cup/90 mL/3 fl oz lukewarm water

1¾ cups/280 g/9 oz pure icing/confectioner's sugar, well sifted

Soak the egg white powder in the water until thoroughly dissolved, approximately 15 minutes. Give the mixture an occasional gentle stir during this time. Strain through a fine sieve into a glass mixing bowl. Add the sugar one spoonful at a time beating well after each addition. Continue adding sugar and beating until the mixture reaches the required consistency.

Note
Both royal icing recipes can be made using an electric mixer but care must be taken not to overbeat which will add too much air to the mixture.

FLOWER MOULDING PASTE

Recipe no 1

- 1 teaspoon powdered gelatine
- 1 teaspoon liquid glucose
- 6 teaspoons/30 mL/1 fl oz water
- $1^1/_2$ cups/230 g/$7^1/_2$ oz pure icing/confectioner's sugar, well sifted
- 1 teaspoon gum tragacanth compound

Soak the gelatine and the glucose in the water for 15-20 minutes then dissolve completely by heating gently over low heat or in a microwave oven. Take care not to overheat and reduce the water content.

Place half the sugar and all the gum tragacanth compound in a glass bowl and stir well to combine. Add the gelatine/glucose mixture to the sugar mixture and stir well. Add small amounts of the extra sugar until the mixture becomes pliable.

Remove from the bowl and knead well. Store in a plastic bag in a sealed container and allow to rest for 30 minutes before using.

A small amount of white fat rubbed on fingers when using paste helps with elasticity.

Cooked sugar syrup is placed on a sugar pump and blown to produce these life-like fruits. *(See page 60.)*

FLOWER MOULDING PASTE (HEATED PASTE)

Recipe no 2

2 level teaspoons powdered gelatine

6 teaspoons/30 mL/1 fl oz water

8 teaspoons/40 mL/approximately 1 large egg white

3 teaspoons pure gum tragacanth

3 cups/460 g/14½ oz pure icing/confectioner's sugar, well sifted

45 g/1½ oz solid white vegetable shortening, completely softened until almost liquid

additional ½ cup/75 g/2½ oz pure icing/confectioner's sugar for kneading

Soak the gelatine in the water for 20-30 minutes. Meanwhile heat half the sugar with all the gum tragacanth in an oven 150°C/300°F/Gas 2 for 15 minutes. Stir the gelatine and water mixture over a gentle heat until the gelatine is completely dissolved.

Add this to the heated sugar mixture together with the egg white. Mix well. Gradually add the remaining sugar until the mixture is smooth and pliable. Remove from the bowl and knead the shortening into the mixture.

Allow to stand for at least twenty-four hours before using. This mixture improves to a very fine paste if it is left for three days before use.

Note

This mixture can be mixed to kneading stage in an electric mixer.

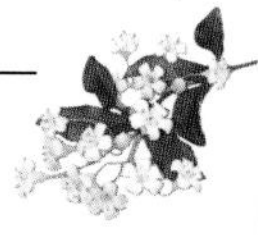

GUM PASTE RECIPE

1 rounded tablespoon gelatine

pinch cream of tartar

1 cup/250 mL/8 fl oz boiling water

13 cups/2 kg/4 lb pure icing/confectioner's sugar

additional $3^1/_4$ cups/500 g/1 lb pure icing/confectioner's sugar

Dissolve the gelatine and cream of tartar in the boiling water. Add to the first amount of sugar and mix to a soft paste. Remove from the bowl and wrap in plastic wrap. Leave for at least two hours in an airtight container then knead in the additional sugar until the desired consistency is reached.

Divide into small amounts and rewrap for later use. This mixture may be frozen for use at later time.

PASTILLAGE

This paste is made using royal icing at soft peak consistency.

4 rounded tablespoons royal icing mixture

1 level teaspoon pure gum tragacanth

additional icing/confectioner's sugar for kneading

Place the royal icing mixture into a small container then add the pure gum tragacanth. Mix well. Cover tightly and place in the refrigerator for two hours.

Sift a small amount of sugar onto a clean surface. Remove the icing mixture from the refrigerator and knead on the icing sugar until the mixture is very pliable. Do not add too much icing sugar at this stage. Cover immediately.

Note
This pastillage is very fast drying so work only with small amounts at any time. If rolling out, dust the surface with cornflour/cornstarch.

INDEX

Page numbers in italics indicate photograph